FIELD GUIDE TO

MS-DOS 6.2

PUBLISHED BY

Microsoft Press
A Division of Microsoft Corporation
One Microsoft Way
Redmond, Washington 98052-6399

Library of Congress Cataloging-in-Publication Data
Field guide to MS-DOS 6.2 / Siechert & Wood.
          p.   cm.
Includes index.
ISBN 1-55615-560-3

1. MS-DOS (Computer file) I. Siechert & Wood, Inc.
QA76.76.063F55   1994
005.4'469--dc20   93-47602
          CIP

Printed and bound in the United States of America.

1 2 3 4 5 6 7 8 9 QBP 9 8 7 6 5 4

Distributed to the book trade in Canada by Macmillan of
Canada, a division of Canada Publishing Corporation.

A CIP catalogue record for this book is available from the
British Library.

Microsoft Press books are available through
booksellers and distributors worldwide. For further
information about international editions, contact your local
Microsoft Corporation office. Or contact Microsoft Press
International directly at fax (206) 936-7329.

Acquisitions Editor: Lucinda Rowley

Project Editor: Tara Powers-Hausmann

Technical Contact: Mary DeJong

Writers: Stan DeGulis, Jim Law, Carl Siechert

FIELD GUIDE TO

MS-DOS 6.2

Siechert & Wood, Inc.

The Field Guide to MS-DOS 6.2 is divided into four sections. These sections are designed to help you find the information you need quickly.

1 ENVIRONMENT

Terms and ideas you'll want to know to get the most out of MS-DOS. All the basic tasks of MS-DOS are shown and explained. The emphasis here is on quick answers, but most topics are cross-referenced so you can find out more if you want to.

Diagrams of key tasks, with quick definitions, cross referenced to more complete information.

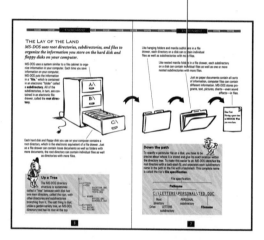

Tipmeister

Watch for me as you use this Field Guide. I'll point out helpful hints and let you know what to watch for.

11 MS-DOS A to Z

An alphabetic list of commands, tasks, terms, and procedures.

Definitions of key concepts and terms, and examples showing you why you should know them.

Cross references to related topics.

Step-by-step guides to performing most MS-DOS tasks.

155 TROUBLESHOOTING

A guide to common problems—how to avoid them, and what to do when they occur.

169 QUICK REFERENCE

Useful indexes, including a full list of menu commands, short-cut keys, and more.

187 INDEX

Complete reference to all elements of the Field Guide.

INTRODUCTION

In the field and on expedition, you need practical solutions. Fast. This field guide provides just these sorts of lightning quick answers. But take two minutes and read the introduction. It explains how this unusual little book works.

HOW TO USE THIS BOOK

Sometime during grade school, my parents gave me a field guide to North American birds. With its visual approach, its maps, and its numerous illustrations, that guide delivered hours of enjoyment. The book also helped me better understand and more fully enjoy the birds in my neighborhood. As an extra bonus the small book fit neatly in a child's rucksack. But I'm getting off the track.

WHAT IS A FIELD GUIDE?

This book works in the same way as that field guide. It organizes information visually with numerous illustrations. And it does this in a way that helps you more easily and more quickly understand working with MS-DOS. For new users, the field guide provides a visual path to finding the essential information necessary to start using MS-DOS. But the field guide isn't only for beginners. For experienced users, the field guide provides concise, easy-to-find descriptions of MS-DOS tasks, terms, and techniques.

WHEN YOU HAVE A QUESTION

Let me explain then how to find the information you need. You'll usually want to flip first to the **Environment** section. The **Environment** works like a visual index. You find the picture that shows what you want to do or the thing you have a question about. If you want to copy a file, for example, you flip to pp. 8-9, since those pages show how you manage files.

Next you read the captions that describe the parts of the picture. Say, for example, you want to know what commands you can use to copy a file. The picture on pp. 8–9 includes a caption that lists the commands for copying files. If you need information on the commands, you can turn to the second section of this book, **MS-DOS A to Z,** where each command is described in detail.

Using **MS-DOS A to Z** is straightforward. **MS-DOS A to Z** resembles a dictionary and alphabetically lists more than 200 entries. The entries define terms and describe commands and tasks. (After you've worked with MS-DOS a bit, you'll often be able to turn directly to **MS-DOS A to Z.**) You can read the **Copy** entry, for example, to learn the different ways you can use the Copy command.

Any time a task or a term from **MS-DOS A to Z** appears, I'll use bold letters for it the first time it appears on a page or in an entry—like I just did for the Copy entry. This way, if you don't understand the term or want to do a bit of brushing up, you can flip to the defined term to get more information.

WHEN YOU HAVE A PROBLEM

The third section of this book, Troubleshooting, describes problems that new or casual users of MS-DOS often encounter. Following each problem description, I list one or more solutions you can use to fix the problem.

WHEN YOU WONDER ABOUT A COMMAND

Near the end of the book are two additional and very useful resources: the **Quick Reference** and the **Index**. The **Quick Reference** describes each of the menu commands and function keys that MS-DOS recognizes. If you want to know what a specific menu command or function key does, turn to the **Quick Reference.** Don't forget about the **Index**. It cross-references all the terms appearing throughout this book.

CONVENTIONS USED HERE

Rather than use wordy phrases such as, "Type the date at the command prompt and then press the Enter key," I'm just going to say, "type the date." When I tell you to *type* something, you'll know it means type and then press the Enter key. No muss. No fuss.

Although this field guide is about MS-DOS version 6 in particular, most of the information here applies to earlier versions of MS-DOS as well. (And when I say MS-DOS version 6, that includes versions 6.0 *and* 6.2.) When something applies only to a particular version of MS-DOS, I'll tell you. Otherwise, you can assume the version of MS-DOS you are using does not matter.

ENVIRONMENT

Need to get the lay of the land quickly? Then the Environment is the place to start. It defines the key terms you'll need to know and the core ideas you should understand as you begin exploring MS-DOS.

WHAT DOES MS-DOS DO?

MS-DOS—an acronym for Microsoft Disk Operating System—is a collection of programs stored on your computer's hard disk. MS-DOS is an essential part of your computer; without it, the various parts of your computer system would be unable to communicate with each other or with you.

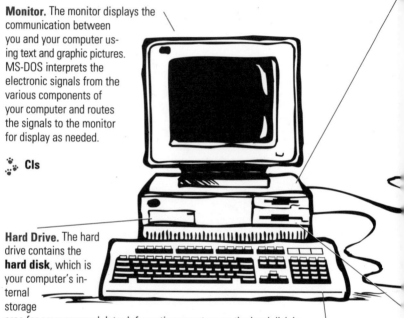

Monitor. The monitor displays the communication between you and your computer using text and graphic pictures. MS-DOS interprets the electronic signals from the various components of your computer and routes the signals to the monitor for display as needed.

⋮ **Cls**

Hard Drive. The hard drive contains the **hard disk**, which is your computer's internal storage area for programs and data. Information you store on the hard disk is permanent and available each time you turn on your computer—unless you choose to erase it. MS-DOS stores, organizes, and retrieves information on the hard disk in response to your commands. These are among MS-DOS's most important functions.

Keyboard. The keyboard is the primary means you use to give commands to your computer. When you press a key on the keyboard, an electronic signal is sent to the system unit. MS-DOS interprets the signal and routes it to the appropriate computer component.

System Unit. The system unit is the heart of your computer. In addition to the **memory** and electronic circuits that make your computer a computer, it contains the **hard drive**, one or more **floppy drives**, and the connectors to which the other parts of your system, such as the monitor, keyboard, mouse, and printer are attached. MS-DOS coordinates and routes information among all of these system components.

⁖ **Mem; MemMaker**

Printer. The printer produces hard copies of information from your computer. MS-DOS routes the information from your computer to the printer for printing.

⁖ **Print; Redirection**

Mouse. The mouse is an alternate way of giving commands to your computer. When you move or click the mouse, an electronic signal is sent to the system unit. MS-DOS interprets the signal and routes it to the appropriate computer component.

Floppy Drive. The **floppy drive** holds the removable storage devices called **floppy disks**. They allow you to load programs onto your computer's **hard disk**, to move information to another computer, and to make copies of information on your hard disk for safe keeping. MS-DOS stores, organizes, and retrieves the information on floppy disks in response to your commands.

STARTING MS-DOS

The process of starting a computer and loading MS-DOS is known as "booting," or "performing a boot," from the phrase "lift yourself up by your bootstraps."

The first activity you see when you **boot** your computer is a self test. Your computer examines its **memory**—its RAM chips—and verifies that they are all working correctly. As it does this, it counts up the memory in **KB** (kilobytes) and displays the count on the screen.

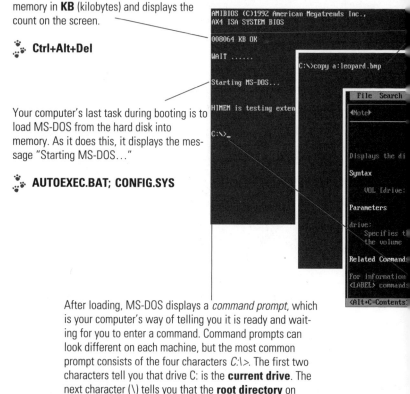

```
AMIBIOS (C)1992 American Megatrends Inc.,
AX4 ISA SYSTEM BIOS

008064 KB OK

WAIT ......
                        C:\>copy a:leopard.bmp
Starting MS-DOS...
                                File  Search
HIMEM is testing exten    ◄Note►

C:\>_                     Displays the di

                          Syntax

                              VOL [drive

                          Parameters

                          drive:
                              Specifies t
                              the volume

                          Related Command:

                          For information
                          <LABEL> command:

                          <Alt+C=Contents>
```

⁂ Ctrl+Alt+Del

Your computer's last task during booting is to load MS-DOS from the hard disk into memory. As it does this, it displays the message "Starting MS-DOS…"

⁂ AUTOEXEC.BAT; CONFIG.SYS

After loading, MS-DOS displays a *command prompt*, which is your computer's way of telling you it is ready and waiting for you to enter a command. Command prompts can look different on each machine, but the most common prompt consists of the four characters *C:\>*. The first two characters tell you that drive C: is the **current drive**. The next character (\) tells you that the **root directory** on drive C is the **current directory**. The last character (>) marks the end of the prompt.

⁂ Prompt

To tell your computer to do something, you type a string of characters at the command prompt and press Enter. Pressing Enter tells the computer you are finished typing and it is OK to proceed. The string of characters you type at the command prompt is called a *command line*. It can be a single word or a group of words. Capitalization doesn't matter. In this Field Guide, we show commands in lowercase letters because it's easier; you can use lowercase or uppercase, or a mixture of the two. However, the order of words and the spaces and punctuation between them is important.

```
                                              Help
  MS-DOS Help: VOL                              1

              VOL

ume label and serial number, if the disk has them.




ve that contains the disk for which you want to display
and serial number.

 assigning a volume label, see the <FORMAT> and

<N=next> <Alt+B=Back>                  N 00001:002
```

You can get help on how to use any command by typing *help* at the command prompt, followed by a space, then the command you want explained.

🐾 **Help**

The flashing underscore to the right of the command prompt is the *cursor*. It identifies the screen position where the next character you type will appear.

Oops!

If you make a typing error at the command prompt, use the Backspace key to erase the error and retype the command. To change your mind and start over, press the Esc key to cancel what you've typed. MS-DOS displays a backslash (\) to show that the command line was canceled, and waits for you to try again.

THE LAY OF THE LAND

MS-DOS uses root directories, subdirectories, and files to organize the information you store on the hard disk and floppy disks on your computer.

MS-DOS uses a system similar to a file cabinet to organize information in your computer. Each time you save information on your computer, MS-DOS puts the information in a "**file**," which is contained in an electronic "folder" called a **subdirectory**. All of the subdirectories, in turn, are contained in an electronic file drawer, called the **root directory.**

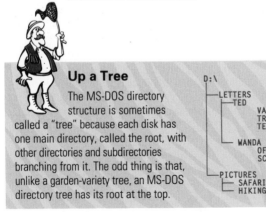

Each hard disk and floppy disk you use on your computer contains a root directory, which is the electronic equivalent of a file drawer. Just as a file drawer can contain loose documents as well as folders with more documents, the root directory can contain individual files as well as directories with more files.

Up a Tree

The MS-DOS directory structure is sometimes called a "tree" because each disk has one main directory, called the root, with other directories and subdirectories branching from it. The odd thing is that, unlike a garden-variety tree, an MS-DOS directory tree has its root at the top.

```
D:\
  ┌─LETTERS
  │   ┌─TED
  │   │     VACATION.DOC
  │   │     TRAVEL.DOC
  │   │     TENTS.DOC
  │   │
  │   └─ WANDA
  │         OFFICE.DOC
  │         SCHEDULE.DOC
  └─PICTURES
      ├─ SAFARI
      └─ HIKING
```

Like hanging folders and manila subfolders in a file drawer, each directory on a disk can contain individual files as well as subdirectories with more files.

Like nested manila folders in a file drawer, each subdirectory on a disk can contain individual files as well as one or more nested subdirectories with more files.

Just as paper documents contain all sorts of information, computer files can contain different information. MS-DOS stores programs, text, pictures, charts—even sound effects—in files.

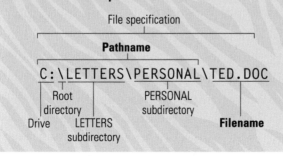

Dear Ted:
Having a great time in MS-DOS. Wish you were here.

Down the path

To specify a particular file on a disk, you have to be precise about where it is stored and give its exact location within the directory tree. To make this easier to do, MS-DOS identifies the root directory with a back-slash (\), and separates each subdirectory name in the path to the file with a backslash. This complete name is called the file's **file specification**.

File specification

Pathname

`C:\LETTERS\PERSONAL\TED.DOC`

Root directory

PERSONAL subdirectory

Drive

LETTERS subdirectory

Filename

MANAGING DISKS AND FILES

Managing disks and files is one of MS-DOS's most important functions. Most MS-DOS commands perform some operation on your hard disk, floppy disks, or your saved files.

MS-DOS provides two commands that let you view a disk's contents—Dir and Tree. The Dir command (short for "directory") displays a list of all the files and subdirectories within the **current directory**. The Tree command displays the names of all of the subdirectories contained in the current directory in a graphic format.

```
Volume in drive C is REDW
Volume Serial Number is 1
Directory of C:\

DOS          <DIR>
WINDOWS      <DIR>
WINWORD      <DIR>
GAMES        <DIR>
CONFIG   SYS          362
COMMAND  COM       54,619
WINA20   386        9,349
AUTOEXEC BAT          359
        8 file(s)          6
                       34,69
```

❖ Dir; Tree

MS-DOS provides commands that let you change the current directory, make a new directory, remove an empty directory, or delete a directory along with its contents.

Changing directories—**CD**

Creating a new directory—**MD**

Removing a directory—**RD; DelTree**

MS-DOS provides commands that let you view, edit, rename, delete, move, copy, and print your files.

Viewing text files—**Type; More**

Editing text files—**Editor**

Renaming files—**Ren**

Deleting files—**Del; Undelete**

Moving files—**Move**

Copying files—**Copy; XCopy; Replace; Backup**

Printing files—**Print**

MS-DOS provides several commands that help you prepare and maintain your floppy disks and your hard disk.

0A39	Preparing a new floppy disk—**Format; Unformat; Sys**
	Checking a disk—**ChkDsk; ScanDisk**
	Copying a floppy disk—**DiskCopy**
09-93 2:42p	Compressing a disk—**DoubleSpace**
09-93 3:21p	Naming a disk—**Label; Vol**
10-93 7:26a	
24-93 1:51p	
05-94 10:31a	
30-93 6:20a	
30-93 6:20a	
04-94 3:59p	
39 bytes	
38 bytes free	

Wildcards

The MS-DOS **wildcard** characters (* and ?) can save you a lot of time and effort when working with files and directories. The asterisk (*) represents any group of characters; the question mark (?) stands for one character in a filename.

MS-DOS
A TO Z

Maybe it's not a jungle out there, but you'll still
want to keep a survival kit close at hand.
MS-DOS A to Z, which starts on the next page,
is just such a survival kit. It lists in alphabetic order
the tools, terms, and techniques
you'll need to know.

. and .. When you view the contents of any **directory** except the **root directory**, you'll see two unusual entries:

```
.              <DIR>
..             <DIR>
```

Each entry represents a directory: The single period represents the **current directory,** and the two periods represent the current directory's **parent directory.** You can use these symbols as shortcuts to specify the directory in a command line. For example, *copy . a:* copies all files from the current directory to drive A. To move all files from the parent directory to the current directory, use this command:

```
move .. .
```

✿ **Dir**

ANSI.SYS

ANSI.SYS is a **device driver** that defines commands for displaying graphics, controlling cursor movement on the screen, and redefining keyboard keys. A few applications require it, but it's unnecessary for most users—except those who want to define a clever, complex command prompt with the **Prompt** command.

Installing ANSI.SYS

If you want ANSI.SYS functions to be available, include this line in your **CONFIG.SYS** file:

```
device=c:\dos\ansi.sys
```

Using ANSI Commands

The easiest way to use ANSI escape sequences—which are listed and explained in **Help** for ANSI.SYS—is with the Prompt command. (Using the Prompt command for this purpose changes the command prompt, so you'll need to restore your usual prompt after using the Prompt command for ANSI codes.) For example, the following sequence of commands changes the F1 key so that it types "help," changes the screen colors to yellow on gray, clears the screen, and restores the default command prompt:

```
prompt $e[0;59;"help "p$e[33;1;47m$e[2J$p$g
prompt $p$g
```

Anti-Virus   A virus is a program written by a ne'er-do-well to prey on unsuspecting users. Some viruses destroy all the data on your hard disk, while others simply display an innocuous message at a predetermined time. Viruses are "contagious"; they typically spread the "infection" when a part of the program copies itself onto every disk or program file it contacts.

Microsoft Anti-Virus is a program (actually two: an MS-DOS–based version and a Windows-based version) that protects your computer from viruses by detecting their presence in memory or on disk and, at your option, eradicating any that it finds. The effect is similar to that of a herd of elephants stomping a mamba snake.

The Windows-based version is more fun because it has pictures of little bugs on the screen, but the two versions are equally effective.

Using Anti-Virus for MS-DOS

To start Microsoft Anti-Virus, type *msav* at the command prompt.

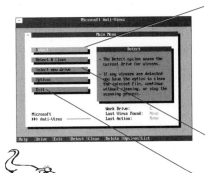

1 Click Detect or press F4 to scan memory and the current drive for viruses. If Anti-Virus finds a virus, it stops to ask what action you want to take. (See "If a Virus Is Found," on the next page.)

2 Click Select New Drive or press F2 to select a different drive to scan.

3 Click Exit or press F3 to quit Anti-Virus.

Before you exit, you might want to perform one of these tasks:

- To display the Options dialog box, click Options or press F8. (For information about the Options dialog box fields, press F1.)

- To delete all the **CHKLIST.MS** files, press F7.

- To display a list of viruses that Anti-Virus can cure, press F9.

continues

A

Anti-Virus *(continued)*

Using Anti-Virus for Windows

To start Microsoft Anti-Virus, double-click the Anti-Virus icon in the
Microsoft Tools program group or choose Antivirus from the **File Manager Tools menu**.

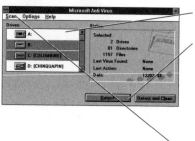

1 Highlight the drive(s) you want to scan.

2 Click Detect to scan memory and the selected drives for viruses. If Anti-Virus finds a virus, it stops to ask what action you want to take. (See "If a Virus Is Found," below.)

3 Choose Exit Anti-Virus from the Scan menu to quit Anti-Virus.

Before you exit, you might want to perform one of these tasks:

• To display the Options dialog box, choose Set Options from the Options menu. (For information about the Options dialog box fields, press F1.)

• To delete all the **CHKLIST.MS** files, choose Delete CHKLIST files from the Scan menu.

• To display a list of viruses that Anti-Virus can cure, choose Virus List from the Scan menu.

If a Virus Is Found

• Click Clean to remove the virus from the infected file. This is normally your best option.

• Click Continue to ignore the finding and continue scanning.

• Click Stop to quit scanning and return to the main Anti-Virus screen.

• Click Delete to erase the infected file from your disk.

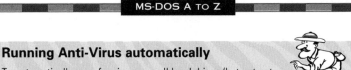

Running Anti-Virus automatically

To automatically scan for viruses on all local drives (but not net-work drives that you use) every time you start your computer, add this line to your **AUTOEXEC.BAT** file:

```
msav /p /l /f
```

    VSafe

Append The Append command allows you to use data files in a specified **directory** as if they were in the **current direc-tory**. It does for data files (that is, documents, spread-sheets, and so on) what the **Path** command does for programs: lets you use them without specifying the com-plete **pathname** every time you need to open them.

Although Append makes it easy to find files, confusion can arise if you make changes to a document and then save it; you might end up with more than one version of the file on your disk. Many programs create a new file (with the same **filename**) in the current directory instead of modifying the existing file in the appended directory. Therefore, *avoid the Append command* except to access files that you view but don't change.

Archive File Attribute   **Attrib; File Attributes**

Assign

The Assign command fools applications into thinking one drive is another, simply by changing its apparent drive letter. Some older programs can run only from drive A or B; with Assign you can put them on your hard disk (drive C) and let the program *think* it's on drive A, for example. Fortunately, these antiquated programs are rare, and today there's little use for Assign. For that reason, it's not included with MS-DOS version 6; if you need it, order the MS-DOS **Supplemental Disk** from Microsoft. (Better yet, get an updated application so that you don't need to use Assign.)

Attrib

The Attrib command displays or changes **file attributes**.

Displaying File Attributes

Type *attrib*, optionally followed by a **file specification**. Attrib displays the name of each file and directory that matches the specification, preceded by a letter for each attribute that is set: *A* (Archive), *S* (System), *H* (Hidden), or *R* (Read-only).

Setting or Clearing File Attributes

For each attribute you want to set, precede its letter with a plus sign (+); for each attribute you want to clear, precede its letter with a minus sign (−). For example, to make all the DOC files in the current directory read-only (so that they cannot be altered), use this command:

```
attrib +r *.doc
```

To set the archive attribute (so that all the DOC files are included in the next backup) and clear the read-only attribute, use this command:

```
attrib +a -r *.doc
```

Extending your reach

To also display or change the file attributes for files in subdirectories of the specified directory, add /S to the command line.

⠿ Dir; Backup

AUTOEXEC.BAT

AUTOEXEC.BAT is a **batch program**—a sequence of MS-DOS commands—that *auto*matically *exec*utes every time you **boot** your computer. AUTOEXEC.BAT is typically used to set up **environment variables**, control the appearance of your display, and start **memory-resident programs** and other applications.

A typical AUTOEXEC.BAT file looks like this:

```
@echo off
cls————————————————————— Clear the screen
c:\dos\smartdrv.exe ————— Load memory-resident
c:\dos\mouse.com                programs
prompt $p$g ————————————— Set the command prompt,
path c:\dos;c:\word;           path, and other
set temp=c:\temp               environment variables
```

Bypassing AUTOEXEC.BAT

If you don't want AUTOEXEC.BAT to run when you start your computer, press F5 when the "Starting MS-DOS..." message appears.

If you want only certain commands in AUTOEXEC.BAT to execute, press F8 when the "Starting MS-DOS..." message appears. MS-DOS then stops at each line in AUTOEXEC.BAT, and asks whether the line should be executed.

If you want only certain commands to execute based upon a menu selection you make, you can use **multiple configurations** and the %CONFIG% environment variable.

These techniques also bypass or selectively execute commands in **CONFIG.SYS,** another file whose commands MS-DOS executes automatically when you start your computer. The techniques are available only in MS-DOS version 6 or later.

Commands typically used in AUTOEXEC.BAT—**Echo; Path; Prompt; Set**

Memory-resident programs you might want to start with AUTOEXEC.BAT—**Doskey; SMARTDrive; VSafe**

Viewing or modifying AUTOEXEC.BAT—**Type; Editor**

Automount

Automount is a feature new to MS-DOS version 6.2 that allows **DoubleSpace** to automatically recognize compressed floppy disks (and other removable media). With version 6.0, you must use the *dblspace /mount* command to read compressed floppy disks. (Use the **Ver** command to find out which version of MS-DOS you have.)

Backup

Backup is a program that archives your files by copying them (in a compressed form) onto floppy disks, network drives, or a removable drive. Use it often!

The program comes in two variants: Microsoft Backup for MS-DOS and Microsoft Backup for Windows. The programs are very similar, and their backup files are identical. Which one you use depends on whether or not you are using Microsoft Windows.

Finding your way

Ever wonder why your computer has a mouse? It's to navigate through programs like Microsoft Backup for MS-DOS. Using it without a mouse is a bit like crossing the ocean without a compass. Sooner or later you'll figure out which direction to go and complete the trip. If you don't have a mouse, these tips for keyboard navigation should point the way:

• To select a rectangular button, use the direction keys to move the highlight. Pressing Enter chooses the button surrounded by inward-pointing triangles—regardless of where the highlight is. The Esc key is a shortcut for the Cancel button; it discards any changes you've made in the current dialog box and closes the box.

• Choosing some buttons brings up a dialog box with a list of options, a list of directories, or a list of files. When the highlight is in a list, press a direction key to move the highlight within the list, press a letter key to move the highlight to the next list item that starts with that letter, or press the Tab key to move the highlight to another dialog box element. Press Spacebar to select the highlighted list item.

Sound confusing? (Yes.) It's not really. It helps to remember that Tab and the direction keys move the highlight, and Spacebar and Enter are "action" keys.

Backing Up Files

To start Microsoft Backup for MS-DOS, type *msbackup* at the command prompt. To start Microsoft Backup for Windows, double-click the Backup icon in Program Manager's **Microsoft Tools program group,** or choose Backup from the **File Manager Tools menu**. The first time you run Backup (either version), it leads you through some configuration steps; simply follow the on-screen instructions. Then follow these steps:

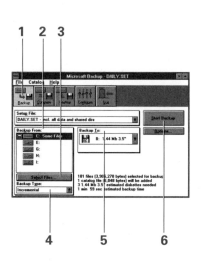

1 Choose the Backup button.

2 To back up all the files on one or more drives, select the drive(s) in the Backup From list.

3 To refine your backup list, choose the Select Files button. Then select the files or directories that you want to include (or exclude) in your backup list. Choose the Special button to limit your selections based on the file creation date or **file attributes**.

4 Select a Backup Type. For more information, see "Types of Backup," below.

5 Select a destination for your backup files in the Backup To list.

6 Backup displays its best estimate of the number of disks and time needed to perform the backup in the lower right corner of the window. Choose the Start Backup button.

continues

Backup *(continued)*

Types of Backup

Backups come in three flavors: Full, Incremental, and Differential. You make your choice in the Backup Type box.

- Full backups include *all* the files that meet your drive- and file-selection criteria.

- Incremental backups include only those files that have been added or changed since your last full or incremental backup—thereby saving time and disks.

- Differential backups include only the files that have been added or changed since the last full backup.

A good strategy is to periodically (say, monthly) do a full backup, and then perform differential backups more frequently—like daily. If you sometimes need to restore an interim version of a file, use a different set of disks for each differential backup.

Setup Files

A setup file, which has the extension SET, contains all the settings you make in the Backup window: which drives and files you want to back up, the type of backup, and the backup destination. Saving the settings in a setup file averts the need to re-create the settings each time you back up. After you have the settings the way you want, pull down the File menu and choose Save Setup As. To reuse the settings in another session, select the file from the Setup File list in the Backup window.

Backup Catalogs

As part of the backup process, Backup creates a backup catalog—a list of all the files included in the backup. Backup saves one copy of the catalog on your hard disk. This copy is saved in the directory specified by the MSDOSDATA **environment variable**, if you specified one, or in the directory containing the Backup program files. Another copy of the backup catalog is saved on the last disk of the backup set.

Backup catalogs have cryptic filenames that include the drive letter of the first and last drives included in the backup set, the date (in the form YMMDD), and a letter that is incremented for each backup performed on a given day. The filename extension indicates the backup type: FUL (full), INC (incremental), or DIF (differential).

The backup catalog contains all the information needed to restore the archived files. If the hard disk copy of the catalog is lost (which, of course, is quite likely when you need it most—such as when your dog accidentally erases all the files on your hard disk), you can retrieve the floppy disk copy or even rebuild the catalog if the floppy disk copy is missing or damaged. To perform either of these tasks in Backup for MS-DOS, choose the Catalog button in the Restore window; in Backup for Windows, choose a command from the Catalog menu.

Restoring Files

This is the part of Backup that you never want to use. Not because it's difficult or dangerous, but you just don't want to be in a situation where you need it! The procedure is similar to backing up:

1 Start Backup and choose the Restore button.

2 Select a backup set catalog.

3 Select the drive containing the backup files.

4 To restore all the files from one or more drives, select the drive(s) in the Restore Files list.

5 To refine your restore list, choose the Select Files button. Then select the files or directories that you want to include (or exclude). Choose the Special button to limit your selections based on the file creation date or **file attributes**.

6 Specify a destination for the restored files.

7 Choose the Start Restore button.

Restoring old backup files

Versions of MS-DOS earlier than 6.0 had a Backup command (not *msbackup*) that, although crude, served the same purpose as the Microsoft Backup program furnished with MS-DOS versions 6.0 and later. If you have backup files that you created with the old Backup command, you can retrieve the information with the **Restore** command; you cannot use the new Microsoft Backup program.

Batch Program

A batch program is a text file that contains a sequence of MS-DOS commands—one command to a line. A batch program (some people call them "batch files") can contain any command that you can type at the command prompt, plus the commands listed below. Use the MS-DOS **Editor** to create or modify a batch program.

The **filename** extension for batch programs is BAT. To run a batch program, you simply type its name—with or without the BAT extension—at the command prompt. MS-DOS executes each of the commands in the file.

Here's what a batch program looks like:

```
@echo off
:begin
if "%1"=="" goto end
echo Copying %1 to drive A
copy %1 a:
shift
goto begin
:end
```

This sample program, which we call 2FLOPPY.BAT, copies files that you specify to the disk in drive A. Unlike the normal **Copy** command, however, this batch program lets you specify several files (or groups of files) on a single command line, like this:

```
2floppy lion.bmp mamba.doc \letters\lost.*
```

AUTOEXEC.BAT is a batch program like any other—except that it automatically runs whenever you start your computer.

❖ Call; Choice; Echo; For; GoTo; If; Pause; Rem; Shift

Booting   Booting is the process your computer goes through when it starts. (It kicks itself so you don't have to.) When you start your computer, either by turning on the power or resetting it after the power is on, it first performs a series of diagnostic tests and then looks for a "bootable" disk—one with operating system files on it. Most PCs look first in drive A, and if there's no disk there, they look to drive C, the first hard drive. After loading the necessary parts of the operating system into memory, MS-DOS takes over the boot process. MS-DOS executes the commands in **CONFIG.SYS** on the boot drive and then runs **AUTOEXEC.BAT**.

When your startup files don't work

If error messages appear (and quickly scroll off the screen) while CONFIG.SYS and AUTOEXEC.BAT execute, or if your system won't boot at all, you might want to bypass these startup files. Press Ctrl+Alt+Del to reboot, and when the "Starting MS-DOS..." message appears, press F5 to bypass CONFIG.SYS and AUTOEXEC.BAT altogether, or press F8 to step through the files one line at a time so you can decide whether or not to execute each line.

🐾 **Ctrl+Alt+Del**

Break   The Break command controls the likelihood that pressing **Ctrl+Break** or **Ctrl+C** can stop a certain process, such as sorting a file. If you use the default Break setting (off), MS-DOS checks to see if you have pressed Ctrl+C only when it reads from the keyboard or writes to the screen or a printer. If you enter *break on* (in **CONFIG.SYS**, use *break=on*), MS-DOS also checks whenever it reads or writes to disk or performs other functions. Break is used most often in CONFIG.SYS and **batch programs,** but you can also use it at the command prompt.

Buffers   The Buffers command specifies the number of disk buffers you want MS-DOS to use. A disk buffer is an area of memory in which MS-DOS saves the information that you most recently read from or wrote to disk—in the hopes that you'll need that information again soon, thereby saving another trip to the hard disk. If you use **SMARTDrive** (which we recommend), set buffers to 10. And even without SMARTDrive, you shouldn't use a value greater than 30. Increasing the number beyond that consumes additional **memory** and doesn't offer any significant speed improvement.

The Buffers command can be used only in **CONFIG.SYS**; you can't enter it at the command prompt. To specify 10 disk buffers, for example, use **Editor** to put this line in CONFIG.SYS:

```
buffers=10
```

Byte   A byte (pronounced the same way as what a lion might take out of you) is computerese for a single character, such as a letter, number, or punctuation symbol. File sizes are measured in bytes, but are often expressed in **KB** (kilobytes) or **MB** (megabytes).

Call   Sometimes you will want a **batch program** to start another batch program. You can do so by simply putting the second program's name in the first program—but any commands in the first program that appear after the second program's name are ignored. With the Call command, however, you can run a second batch program, and when it finishes running, MS-DOS continues running the first program with the line following the Call command. For example, if you have a batch-program menuing system in which you want to run another batch program called COPY-ALL.BAT, include this line in the MENU.BAT file:

```
call copy-all
```

CD

The CD command—short for "Change Directory"—displays or sets the **current directory**. To display the name of the current directory, simply type *cd*. To change the current directory, add the name of the directory you want to change to. For example:

```
cd \word\letters
```

Saving a few keystrokes

You don't need to type the complete path to a directory; you need only specify the *relative* path from the current directory. For example, if the current directory is \WORD, you can type *cd letters* to change to \WORD\LETTERS. You can also use the . **and** .. directory entries. To change back to the \WORD directory (the **parent directory** of the current directory), use this command:

```
cd ..
```

CD-ROM Drive

CD-ROM, which stands for "Compact Disc–Read Only Memory" is a popular medium for distributing large amounts of data, such as encyclopedias, telephone directories, and multimedia adventures packed with sights and sounds. Using a CD-ROM drive requires some additions to your startup files.

1 In your **CONFIG.SYS** file, you must include a **Device** (or **DeviceHigh**) command that loads a **device driver** for your CD-ROM drive. (You get the device driver—and instructions for installing it, you hope!—with your CD-ROM drive.)

2 In your **AUTOEXEC.BAT** file, include an **Mscdex** command.

After you have taken these steps, you access the CD-ROM drive exactly the same way you access a hard drive or floppy drive.

Speeding up CD-ROM access with SMARTDrive

No CD-ROM drive—including the new double-speed or triple-speed models—is as fast at retrieving data as a good hard drive. But a software disk cache (**SMARTDrive** comes to mind) improves data throughput significantly. SMARTDrive caching of CD-ROM drives has two requirements: You must use MS-DOS version 6.2 (the SMARTDrive included with earlier versions doesn't cache CD-ROM drives), and you must place the Mscdex line *before* the SMARTDrive line in your AUTOEXEC.BAT file.

ChDir   CD

ChkDsk   The ChkDsk command reports information about a disk (such as the disk's total space, free space, and number of directories and files) and, optionally, can "repair" any disk errors it finds. (We use the term *repair* loosely because, although ChkDsk can recover space occupied by corrupted files, it can't restore those files in a format that's generally useful.) To use ChkDsk, at the command prompt type *chkdsk*. You'll see a report something like this:

```
D:\>chkdsk

Volume DELPHINIUM  created 07-17-1993 4:34p
Volume Serial Number is 1B69-7DE2

    169,750,528 bytes total disk space
    122,015,744 bytes in 3 hidden files
         45,056 bytes in 11 directories
     45,580,288 bytes in 237 user files
      2,109,440 bytes available on disk

          4,096 bytes in each allocation unit
         41,441 total allocation units on disk
            513 available allocation units on disk

        655,360 total bytes memory
        614,128 bytes free

Instead of using CHKDSK, try using SCANDISK.  SCANDISK can reliably detect
and fix a much wider range of disk problems.  For more information,
type HELP SCANDISK from the command prompt.

D:\>
```

Take the following steps if the ChkDsk report includes a message similar to this:

```
45 lost allocation units found in 1 chains.
     368,640 bytes disk space would be freed
```

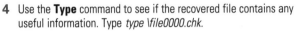

C

1   Type *chkdsk /f.*

2   Answer *Y* when ChkDsk asks if you want to repair the disk.

3   ChkDsk collects the loose ends ("lost allocation units") and stores them in the **root directory** in files with names like **FILE0000.CHK**. Type *dir *.chk* to see a list of the files.

4   Use the **Type** command to see if the recovered file contains any useful information. Type *type \file0000.chk.*

5   If you can't read the information, simply delete the file. Type *del \file*.chk.* There is nothing else you can do with these files, and you haven't recovered the disk space until the files are gone.

ScanDisk

CHKLIST.MS   You might notice a file named CHKLIST.MS in each of your directories; **Anti-Virus** creates it when it scans for viruses. CHKLIST.MS stores information about each file in the directory; when you run Anti-Virus again, it checks to see if any files in the directory have changed (which could indicate a possible virus infection).

Regaining some disk space

You can safely delete the CHKLIST.MS files to save disk space. You can do so within Anti-Virus: While it's running, simply press F7. (If you're using Anti-Virus for Windows, choose Delete CHKLIST files from the Scan menu.) To prevent Anti-Virus from re-creating CHKLIST.MS files, open the Options dialog box and be sure that Verify Integrity and Create New Checksums are not checked.

Choice

The Choice command lets you ask the user to make a choice while a **batch program** runs, and then execute certain commands based on the user's choice. It's useful only in batch programs—not at the command prompt.

Specifying the Choices

You specify the valid choices with the /C switch. For example, the line *choice /c:ynq* causes MS-DOS to display:

```
[Y, N, Q]?
```

MS-DOS waits patiently until the user presses one of those three letters. Choice then sets the **ErrorLevel** to the number that corresponds with the letter: 1 for the first letter choice, 2 for the second choice, and so on. You can also specify a default choice—a selection that's made automatically if the user doesn't make a choice within a specified time—with the /T switch. And you can add an explanatory prompt. Changing the example above to *choice /c:ynq /t:q,30 Yes, No, or Quit* produces this display:

```
Yes, No, or Quit [Y, N, Q]?
```

If the user doesn't respond within 30 seconds, Choice acts as if the user pressed Q.

Explaining the choices

You can use the **Echo** command to display one or more lines of descriptive text—or perhaps a lengthy menu of choices—that better explain the choices presented by the Choice command. Simply precede the Choice command with appropriate Echo commands, like this:

```
@echo off
echo Type the first letter of the best musician:
echo    Beatles
echo    Frank Sinatra
echo    LL COOL J
echo    Mozart
echo    Pearl Jam
echo    You call these musicians???
choice /c:bflmpy /n Enter letter:
```

If

Cls   The Cls command clears the screen and then displays the command prompt.

Code Page   As you explore the world, you'll likely see accented characters and other symbols that don't appear on your keyboard. MS-DOS can replace some of the 256 U.S.–standard characters with characters more likely to be used in other countries. Each country-specific set of characters is called a *code page*. The MS-DOS Setup program makes the appropriate settings for the country you specify when you install MS-DOS. If you want to change to a different code page, you'll need to pore through online **Help** for the following commands, which aren't covered in this *Field Guide*: Chcp, Country, DISPLAY.SYS, Keyb, Mode, and NLSFunc.

Command   The Command command starts the MS-DOS command processor, the program that recognizes and performs MS-DOS commands. You'll probably never need to use the Command command, because the command processor loads automatically when you **boot** your computer or double-click the MS-DOS Prompt icon in Windows. You might find it used in some older **batch programs**, but that functionality has been supplanted by the **Call** command.

⁂ **Exit**

Command History ⁙ Doskey

Comp The Comp command compares two files—but it's a relic of MS-DOS versions 5.0 and earlier. Use the **FC** command instead.

CONFIG.SYS

CONFIG.SYS is a file that contains commands that configure your computer. The file, which must be in the **root directory**, is executed automatically whenever you **boot** your computer. It typically contains commands that install **device drivers** for various system components, configure **memory**, establish certain default settings, and other esoterica.

```
device=c:\dos\himem.sys  /m:1          Configure memory
device=c:\dos\emm386.exe  noems
dos=high, umb
buffers=10,0                           Other esoterica
files=80
lastdrive=z                            Install device drivers
devicehigh /1:1,9072 =c:\dos\ansi.sys
devicehigh /1:1,39488 =c:\dos\dblspace.sys /move
```

With the exception of **Device** and **DeviceHigh** commands, the order of commands in CONFIG.SYS is unimportant. (You must group the commands for each configuration in a startup menu, but the order of commands within the groups doesn't matter.)

To view or change your CONFIG.SYS file, use **Editor**. (Because CONFIG.SYS is executed only when you boot the computer, you must restart the computer for your changes to take effect.)

Running Specific CONFIG.SYS Commands

MS-DOS versions 6.0 and later offer three ways to control which CONFIG.SYS commands run when your computer starts:

- When the "Starting MS-DOS..." message appears, press F8. MS-DOS then pauses to ask whether each command in CONFIG.SYS (and **AUTOEXEC.BAT**) should be executed. This method is useful for the rare occasion when you don't want to load a certain driver, for example.

- Set up **multiple configurations** with a startup menu. MS-DOS displays the menu so you can decide which group of commands to execute. This is useful when you have two or more configurations that you frequently switch between. (For example, you might sometimes want to install network drivers so you can use shared devices, and other times avoid the network to obtain more working memory—like when you want to play games.)

- Insert a question mark immediately after a command name so that MS-DOS stops to ask you whether to run that command each time you start your computer. For example, to confirm whether to load a mouse driver (you don't need to load a mouse driver if you are working in Windows, which provides its own driver), use this command: *devicehigh?=c:\mouse\mouse.sys*. If your multiple configurations are identical except for the addition of one or two drivers, this method is simpler than creating a startup menu.

Using descriptive comments in CONFIG.SYS

Many CONFIG.SYS commands are incomprehensible to people who speak only English. You might find it useful to add explanatory notes to your file (when you figure out what it does!). Your comments must be on a separate line; you can't add them to a command line. Simply precede the comment with **Rem** (for "remark") or a semicolon (;). These comment identifiers must be placed at the beginning of the line. You can also add blank lines to improve the readability of your CONFIG.SYS file.

CONFIG.SYS commands used to create multiple configurations—
Include; MenuColor; MenuDefault; MenuItem; Submenu

Commands used only in CONFIG.SYS—**Buffers; Device; DeviceHigh; DOS; Files; Install; LastDrive; NumLock; Shell; Stacks**

Other commands that can be used in CONFIG.SYS—**Break; Rem; Set; Verify**

Copy   The Copy command can combine several files into a
single file, print files, create text files, and perform other
seldom-used functions, but its raison d'être is to copy one
or more files from one directory or drive to another. In
its simplest form, you specify the name of a file to copy,
and Copy makes a copy of the file in the **current directory**. For example, if drive C is the **current drive**, typing
copy a:letter.doc copies the file named LETTER.DOC on
drive A to the current directory on drive C.

More commonly, you'll specify both a source and a
destination for the copy operation. For example:

```
copy a:love-ltr.doc c:\wp\letters
```

This command copies LOVE-LTR.DOC from drive A to
the LETTERS directory on drive C.

- If you don't specify a destination **filename**, Copy
  creates a file in the destination directory with the same
  filename, date, and time as the original file.

- If the LETTERS directory doesn't exist, MS-DOS
  interprets it as a filename, so the file is copied to the
  WP directory and renamed as LETTERS.

Which brings us to another point: You can use Copy to
rename files as you copy them. If relations turn sour, for
example, type *copy love-ltr.doc hate-ltr.doc* to make a copy
of the original file and rename it. (To rename a file
without making a copy of it, use the **Ren** command
instead.)

Of course, you can use **wildcard** characters in the **file
specification**, which allows you to copy several files with a
single command—like this one, which copies all files in
the current directory with a DOC extension to the
ARCHIVE directory:

```
copy *.doc c:\archive
```

With MS-DOS versions 6.0 and earlier, if a file with the name you specify already exists in the destination directory, Copy simply replaces it with the source file—obliterating the old file in the destination directory. Beginning with version 6.2, Copy warns you if the copy operation you've requested will wipe out an existing file, and gives you an opportunity to reconsider. (If you don't want to be bothered with such safety features, add /Y to the Copy command line.)

Changing a file's creation date and time

Here's an arcane, but sometimes handy, trick: To change the date and time that appear in a file's directory entry, use the /B switch and the punctuation shown below. This command makes a new copy of the file (in the same location, and with the same name) and gives it the current date and time.

```
copy /b love-ltr.doc+,,
```

 **XCopy; Move; Replace**

Copying MS-DOS includes several commands to help you copy. What do you want to copy?

Disks—**DiskCopy**

Files and directories—**Copy; Replace; XCopy; Backup**

Files from the original MS-DOS disks—**Expand**

Ctrl+Alt+Del   This key combination—affectionately known as the three-fingered salute—causes the computer system to **boot**, or restart. It's sometimes necessary to tame an unruly application—such as one that locks up your computer. You should use it only as a last resort; first try the application's normal exit command. (Well, second-to-last resort: If Ctrl+Alt+Del won't restart the computer, try the computer's reset button. And if that doesn't work, it's time for the ultimate restart—the on/off switch.) Pressing these keys is perfectly safe if you are at the command prompt, but if an application is running when you restart the computer, you'll probably lose whatever information you were working on at that time.

Ctrl+Break   This key combination can sometimes stop runaway processes—such as unexpectedly long **Dir** listings or files you display with **Type**. Whether you can successfully stop such operations depends on the setting of the **Break** command and the application you are trying to stop. Most applications don't pay any attention to the Ctrl+Break key combination, but it is effective for interrupting many MS-DOS commands. You can also use Ctrl+Break to cancel a command on the command line before you press Enter.

On most keyboards, Break shares a key with Pause, and it's usually located in the upper right corner of the keyboard. Pressing the key by itself pauses the display; pressing the key while holding down the Ctrl key produces a Ctrl+Break.

Ctrl+C   In many instances, pressing the Ctrl+C key combination produces the same result as **Ctrl+Break:** It stops the current process or cancels the current command. Don't be too disappointed if it doesn't work, however. In most **Windows-based applications,** as well as many newer **MS-DOS–based applications,** Ctrl+C copies the current selection to the Clipboard (or an equivalent data "holding pen"). And in other applications, Ctrl+C performs a completely different function—or does nothing at all.

Current Directory   Every traveler has to be someplace, and the current directory is where you "are." The current directory is the one that is currently active, and any commands you enter affect files in this directory (unless you precede the **filename** with a **pathname**). The command prompt usually displays the name of the current directory. To make a different directory the current directory (or to see where you are if the command prompt doesn't show the current directory), use the **CD** command.

   Current Drive

Current Drive   The current drive is the one that is currently active. The **current directory** on the current drive gets all MS-DOS's attention unless you explicitly specify another. (Do you feel like you're getting caught in the "currents"?) When you type the name of a file as part of an MS-DOS command, for example, MS-DOS assumes the file exists in the current directory on the current drive unless you specify otherwise. If you precede the **filename** with a drive letter and a colon (but no backslash), MS-DOS looks for the file in the current directory on the specified drive.

The letter of the current drive, which can be any **floppy drive**, hard drive, **CD-ROM drive**, and so on, is usually displayed as part of the command prompt. To make a different drive the current drive, type the new drive letter followed by a colon at the command prompt and press Enter. For example, to make drive D the current drive, enter:

```
d:
```

CVF   A CVF (Compressed Volume File) is a file that contains a **DoubleSpace** "drive." A DoubleSpace-compressed drive is not an actual physical drive; it's merely a file that looks and acts like a drive. A CVF, which has read-only, hidden, and system **file attributes**, is stored in the **root directory** of a host drive (an actual drive) and has a filename like DBLSPACE.000. Because of the compression capabilities of DoubleSpace, a compressed drive usually contains much more data than the size of the CVF suggests.

Date

The Date command displays and lets you set the date in your computer's system clock. MS-DOS uses the system clock to "stamp" the current time and date on a file's directory entry whenever you create or modify a file. Programs such as **Backup** and **XCopy** can use a file's date to decide which files to process. In addition, applications such as personal information managers and personal finance programs use the system clock to remind you of appointments and bills due.

Using the Date Command

Simply type *date* at the command prompt. MS-DOS responds:

```
Current date is Mon 03-14-1994
Enter new date (mm-dd-yy):
```

If the date displayed is correct, press Enter. To change the date, type the correct date and press Enter.

Does the date look backward to you?

By default, MS-DOS displays dates in *mm-dd-yyyy* format. If your roots are outside the United States, however, a different order (such as *dd-mm-yyyy* or *yyyy-mm-dd*) or a different separator (a slash or a period) might look more familiar to you. To change the date format, add a command like this to your **CONFIG.SYS** file:

```
country=033,,c:\dos\country.sys
```

Replace 033 with the country code for the country you want to use. You can find a list of the supported countries, their codes, and the date and time format in online **Help** for the Country command, but here's a hint: For most countries, the country code is the same as the telephone country code.

Time

Debug   Debug is primarily a tool for programmers and other techies to explore and test programs—but you might occasionally have a use for it: Some computer magazines publish small utility programs that can be easily entered with Debug. Fortunately, the details you need for that process are few, and they're usually well explained by the magazine.

Defrag   The Defrag program "optimizes" your disk by rearranging its files and directories so they can be accessed most quickly. When you create a file on a disk, MS-DOS stores it in the first available space—including "holes" that have been left by the deletion of other files. If the entire file won't fit in the hole, MS-DOS places as much as possible there, and places the rest in the next available disk space. Over time, the process of creating, modifying, and deleting files results in a patchwork of unconnected file segments. Defrag simply reassembles the various snippets into a single contiguous block.

Using Defrag

1   To start Microsoft Defrag, at the command prompt type *defrag.*

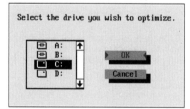

```
Select the drive you wish to optimize.

    A:          ↑
    B:                    OK
    C:
    D:                  Cancel
                ↓
```

2   Use the Up or Down direction key to select a drive and then press Enter.

3 Defrag cogitates briefly and displays a recommendation. Choose Optimize to perform the recommended optimization method. (Or choose Configure to choose other options, and then press Alt+B to begin optimization.)

```
┌─Optimize──────────────────────────────────────Esc=Stop Defrag─┐
│ XX                        X                                    │
│                                                                │
│                                                                │
│                                                                │
│ X                                                              │
│                    X                                           │
│  XXXXXXXXXXXXXXXXXXXXXXXXXXXXXXXXXXXX                           │
│        X X                                                     │
│                                                                │
├──Status──────────────────────┬──Legend──────────────────────  │
│ Cluster 2,100          4%     │ ▓ - Used       ▒ - Unused      │
│ ▓                             │ r - Reading    W - Writing     │
│     Elapsed Time: 00:01:11    │ B - Bad        X - Unmovable   │
│        Full Optimization      │ Drive C:  1 block = 50 clusters│
├──────────────────────────────┴───────────────────────────────┤
│ Sorting...                              │ Microsoft Defrag     │
└───────────────────────────────────────────────────────────────┘
```

A shortcut to Defrag

You can bypass the disk selection and recommendation screens by adding the letter of the drive you want to optimize to the command line. In addition, you can use the /S switch to specify the order in which you want the files to be arranged. This command, for example, tells Defrag to optimize drive C, sorting the files and directories first by extension, and then by filename:

```
defrag c: /s:en
```

:::. **DoubleSpace**

Del

Del (short for "delete") deletes one or more files from your disk. Add the **file specification** to the command line and poof! They're gone. To delete all your 1992 expense reports, for example, enter *del \expense\92*.xls*.

Playing it safe

Unless you enter a command that would delete all the files in a directory (such as *del .* or *del \expense*.**), MS-DOS quickly deletes the specified file(s) without further ado. If you add the /P switch to the command line, however, Del displays the name of each file it proposes to eradicate, and awaits your approval. Press Y to confirm the deletion, N to cancel the deletion and display the next filename (if you specified a group of files), or **Ctrl+C** to stop the Del command.

Deleting directories—**DelTree; RD**

Erasing a disk—**Format**

Recovering deleted files—**Undelete; Delete Sentry; Delete Tracker**

Delete Sentry

Delete Sentry is the highest form of protection offered by **Undelete**. If you have Delete Sentry enabled, you should have no problem recovering files that you accidentally delete. (Even with Delete Sentry, however, you must discover and correct your error quickly; files protected with Delete Sentry are normally purged seven days after they are deleted.)

To enable Delete Sentry protection for files on drive C, add this line to your **AUTOEXEC.BAT** file:

```
undelete /s
```

Why doesn't everyone use Delete Sentry?

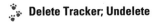

The protection provided by Delete Sentry is not without cost. First, because Delete Sentry actually saves your deleted files in a hidden directory, those deleted files continue to occupy disk space—as if they had never been deleted. (Delete Sentry purges the oldest files in its directory so that it never occupies more than about 20 percent of your total disk space.) If your disk is nearly full, you might not want to use Delete Sentry.

Second, Undelete must run as a **memory-resident program** to enable Delete Sentry, and it therefore uses about 13 **KB** of **memory**. If you cannot run some programs because you don't have enough free memory, run **MemMaker**; it might be able to load Undelete into an unused part of high memory.

Delete Tracker; Undelete

Delete Tracker   Delete Tracker is the second of three levels of protection offered by **Undelete**. Delete Tracker saves information about files you delete, but unlike **Delete Sentry**, Delete Tracker does not save the actual files. Therefore, to successfully undelete a file when Delete Tracker is enabled, you must do so before MS-DOS places another file in the space occupied by the deleted file. There's no accurate way to know when that will be, so the best solution is to undelete accidentally deleted files *as soon as possible*.

To enable Delete Tracker protection for files on drive C, add this line to your **AUTOEXEC.BAT** file:

```
undelete /tc
```

Delete Sentry; Undelete

Deloldos   Disk full? One likely culprit is the **OLD_DOS.1** directory that Setup creates when you upgrade from an earlier
MS-DOS version. If your computer seems to be working
properly, you shouldn't ever need to "downgrade" to that
earlier version. Deloldos to the rescue! Type *deloldos* at
the command prompt, and Deloldos removes
OLD_DOS.1 (and OLD_DOS.2, OLD_DOS.3, etc. if you
upgraded more than once) and as a final step, removes
the Deloldos program itself from your hard drive, because you won't need it again. Another thing you won't
need is the Uninstall disk that Setup created for you;
without the OLD_DOS.1 directory, it's useless.

🐾 **Uninstall**

DelTree   Be careful with this one! The DelTree command deletes
an entire "branch" of your directory tree—including all
the files and subdirectories (and their files) in the directory you specify. DelTree is voracious: It even eradicates
files with read-only, system, or hidden **file attributes**
without hesitation.

This example deletes the \OLDSTUFF directory and all
files and subdirectories contained within it:

```
deltree \oldstuff
```

Before DelTree does its dirty deed, it asks if you want to
delete the directory and all its subdirectories. Read the
name of the directory in the message. Then read it again.
Read it a third time. If you're positive you want to delete
it, press Y; otherwise press N.

Deleting directories—**RD**

Deleting files—**Del**

Recovering deleted files and directories—**Undelete; Delete
Sentry; Delete Tracker**

Device   The Device command is used in a **CONFIG.SYS** file to
load a **device driver**. A typical CONFIG.SYS file has several Device commands. The order of Device commands
in CONFIG.SYS is important for two reasons:

- First, some device drivers depend on the existence of
  certain other drivers, and therefore can be successfully
  installed only if the other driver is already running. For
  example, you must load **HIMEM.SYS** before you load
  any device driver that uses extended memory or high
  memory, such as **EMM386.EXE**. Similarly, some
  networks require that their device drivers are loaded in
  a specific order.

- Second, by loading device drivers in a certain order (as
  long as you obey the foregoing restrictions), you can
  make more efficient use of free **memory** by shoehorning
  device drivers into otherwise unused sections of memory. MS-DOS includes a tool for figuring out the best
  loading order for efficient memory use: **MemMaker**.

A device command in CONFIG.SYS includes the name of
the device driver file. Some device drivers also require
additional information following the **file specification**.
(Check the documentation or online **Help** for the device
driver—not the Device command—to learn about the
additional information needed.) A typical Device
command looks like this:

```
device=c:\dos\ramdrive.sys 1024 /e
```

Device Driver   A device driver provides information to MS-DOS about a certain hardware component, or device. Your computer's keyboard, mouse, monitor, printer, disk drives, and expansion cards are all devices. MS-DOS has built-in device drivers to handle many devices, including the keyboard, disk drives, and monitor; you can use these devices without installing a separate device driver. Installable device drivers, however, can be used to support devices for which MS-DOS has no built-in support—and to support custom features (such as foreign language characters) in the standard devices. MS-DOS includes the following installable device drivers:

ANSI.SYS	**HIMEM.SYS**
CHKSTATE.SYS	**INTERLNK.EXE**
DBLSPACE.SYS	**POWER.EXE**
(DoubleSpace)	**RAMDRIVE.SYS**
DISPLAY.SYS	**SETVER.EXE**
DRIVER.SYS	SMARTDRV.EXE
EGA.SYS	**(SMARTDrive)**
EMM386.EXE	

You can find information about these device drivers in this *Field Guide* and in online **Help**. Other devices that you attach to your computer—such as a mouse, **CD-ROM drive,** or scanner—are furnished with a device driver; the documentation for the device should explain how to install and use the driver.

⁂ **Device; DeviceHigh; Device Names**

DeviceHigh   The DeviceHigh command, like the **Device** command, is used in a **CONFIG.SYS** file to load a **device driver.** The difference between Device and DeviceHigh is that Device always loads device drivers into conventional **memory** (the area you would like to keep free to run programs), whereas DeviceHigh attempts to load drivers into the upper memory area. (If upper memory is not available, DeviceHigh functions exactly like Device.)

For the DeviceHigh command to work, your computer must have extended memory (a computer with a 386, 486, or Pentium processor and more than 1 **MB** of RAM has extended memory) and the following lines must be in your CONFIG.SYS file *before* any DeviceHigh commands:

```
device=c:\dos\himem.sys
device=c:\dos\emm386.exe
dos=umb
```

Using DeviceHigh most effectively

You can use /L and /S switches with DeviceHigh to specify exactly how and where device drivers should load—but this fine-tuning is best done by **MemMaker**.

 LoadHigh

Device Name　Many standard devices attached to your computer have a device name by which they can be addressed. These names are used in programs (to select an output device, for example) as well as in MS-DOS commands. MS-DOS reserves the following names for devices; you cannot use them for **filenames**.

LPT1	First parallel printer port
LPT2–LPT4	Additional parallel printer ports
PRN	Default printer port (normally LPT1)
COM1	First serial communications port
COM2–COM4	Additional serial communications ports
AUX	Default communications port (normally COM1)
NUL	"Null" device, typically used as a destination for messages you don't want to see
CON	Console (keyboard and monitor)

Diagnostics　∴ MSD

Dir　The Dir command displays a list of the files and subdirectories in the **directory** you specify. A typical directory listing looks like this:

```
B:\>dir

 Volume in drive B is CS_TRANSFER
 Volume Serial Number is 12F2-1728
 Directory of B:\

FGD-FG1  BAK     17,484 11-11-93   5:34p
DOS-OUTL DOC     19,174 11-09-93   4:30p
BIO      DOC      1,536 07-27-88   5:44p
FGD-FG2  DOC     26,112 12-07-93   5:45a
MWAV-ICO BMP      1,150 11-23-93   6:29p
VNB      386     41,457 02-11-93   7:01p
EXTEN    DOC      6,656 11-27-93   2:40p
MWAV     BMP     71,030 11-23-93   7:06p
FGD-FG1  DOC    297,984 12-09-93   3:54p
CHKDSK   TXT        861 11-28-93  11:51p
       10 file(s)       483,444 bytes
                        241,664 bytes free
```

— Disk's **volume label**
— Name of directory
— **Filename**
— File size (in **bytes**)
— Date file was created or last modified
— Time file was created or last modified
— Number of files and total size of files listed
— Amount of free space on the disk

Printing a directory listing

You can use **redirection** to direct the output of the Dir command to your printer instead of to the screen. To do so, add > *prn* to the end of the command line. For example,

```
dir *.exe /o > prn
```

prints an alphabetical list of all files with an EXE extension in the **current directory**.

Controlling Which Files Appear in a Dir Listing

You can include a **file specification** with a Dir command so that the listing includes only files that match the specification. For example, to limit the listing to show files in the current directory that have a filename starting with the letter B and a DOC or DOT extension, use this command:

```
dir b*.do?
```

The /S switch extends the command to include all files in the specified directory and all its subdirectories.

You can use the /A switch to restrict the directory listing to those files that have (or don't have) the **file attributes** you specify. Follow the /A with one or more of the following:

A	To include only files with the archive attribute (files that need to be backed up)
H	To include only files with the hidden attribute
R	To include only files with the read-only attribute
S	To include only files with the system attribute
D	To show directories

To include only files that do not have a certain attribute, precede the letter with a minus sign. Similarly, to exclude directories (that is, show files only), use –D.

You can combine these attribute switches. When you do so, Dir displays only those files that match all your criteria. For example, to search an entire disk to find all non–read-only files that need to be backed up, type this:

```
dir \*.* /a-ra /s
```

continues

Dir *(continued)*

If you want it all

Use the /A switch without any other letters to display *all* files that match the specification—including system and hidden files. To see all files in a directory, type *dir /a*.

Controlling the Appearance of a Dir Listing

The Dir command also has several switches that control the appearance of directory listings:

/P	Pauses the listing after each screenful
/O	Determines the order that files and directories are listed; follow /O with N (to sort by filename), E (extension), D (date), S (size), and/or G (to group directories first)
/L	Displays filenames and directory names in lowercase letters
/W	Wide format; includes filenames and directory names only, five per line
/B	"Bare" format; includes filenames and pathnames only, one per line (no heading, summary information, sizes, or dates)

You can use more than one letter after the /O (order) switch to perform a multilevel sort. For example, to sort first on date and then by filename within each date, use /ODN. You can reverse the normal sort order by preceding a letter with a minus sign. For example, to group directories last (instead of first), use /O–G.

Creating your own default Dir settings

If you want to see directory listings sorted by extension and then by name, and you want the display to pause after each screenful, you need to include */oen /p* on the command line each time you use Dir. The DIRCMD **environment variable** can be used to store default switches for the Dir command—ones that you always want to use unless you explicitly use a different switch combination. Add the following line to your **AUTOEXEC.BAT** file, and Dir acts as if you typed */oen /p*:

```
set dircmd=/oen /p
```

You can use any valid Dir switches—or even a file specification—in the DIRCMD environment variable.

 Wildcard

Directory   MS-DOS keeps track of the files on a disk by maintaining a directory, or list, of the files. The directory includes the name of each file, the time and date the file was created or last modified, the size of the file, and its location on the disk.

Each disk has a **root directory**, which is the disk's primary directory. Disks may also have other directories, sometimes called subdirectories, that branch out from the root directory.

So that you don't have to specify the entire directory path every time you refer to a file, MS-DOS lets you make one directory on each drive the active, or **current directory**. MS-DOS always assumes that you are referring to the current directory when you specify a **filename** without a **pathname**.

MS-DOS includes several commands for managing directories and the files they include:

Copying—**XCopy; Backup; Replace**
Creating—**MD**
Including in the search path—**Path; Append**
Moving—**Move**
Removing—**DelTree; RD**
Renaming—**Move**
Selecting—**CD**
Viewing—**Dir; Tree**

Disk Cache ⠿ **SMARTDrive**

DiskComp   The DiskComp command compares two **floppy disks** to see if they are identical. It compares the disks track by track (data is stored on a disk in concentric rings, called tracks) rather than file by file. So even if the two disks contain exactly the same files, if the files aren't laid out on the disk in exactly the same way, DiskComp reports that the disks are not identical.

DiskComp works only with floppy disks, and the two disks you want to compare must be of the same type (for example, both 3½-inch high density).

To compare the disk in drive A with the disk in drive B, use this command:

```
diskcomp a: b:
```

If you have only one drive

You can still use the DiskComp and DiskCopy commands even if you have only one floppy drive for the disk size you want to use. Specify the same drive twice (for example, *diskcomp a: a:*) and MS-DOS prompts you to swap disks when it needs to work with the disk that's not currently in the drive. Depending on the capacity of the disks you are working with, the amount of free space on your hard disk, and the amount of free memory, you might be asked to swap several times before the operation is complete.

FC

DiskCopy   The DiskCopy command copies the contents of an entire **floppy disk** to another floppy disk. To use the command, specify the letters of the drives that contain the source (original) and destination (copy) disks, like this:

```
diskcopy a: b:
```

The two disks you want to use (the source and the destination) must be of the same type (for example, both 3½-inch high density). The destination disk does not need to be formatted; DiskCopy formats the disk as it copies.

   Copy; XCopy

Disk Drive   A disk drive is the contraption that reads and writes disks, which store information—programs, data files, documents, images, and so on. Unlike **memory**, disks retain their information after the computer's power is off. A typical computer system has one or two **floppy drives** and one or more hard drives. The first floppy drive is called drive A. (And if you have only one floppy drive, it's also called B. Go figure.) The first hard drive is called C; the letters D through Z are used to identify additional hard drives, **CD-ROM drives**, **RAMDrives**, **Interlnk** connections, or network drives. Whenever you use a drive's letter in a command or as part of a **file specification**, you must place a colon (:) after the letter. As you would expect of a *disk* operating system, MS-DOS includes several disk-related commands:

Archiving—**Backup**

Checking a disk's integrity—**ChkDsk; ScanDisk**

Compressing—**DoubleSpace**

Copying—**DiskCopy**

Naming—**Label; Vol**

Preparing for use—**FDisk; Format; Sys**

Removing files—**Del; DelTree; Format**

DOS   The DOS command enables two features that leave more conventional **memory** free for programs to use:

- It specifies whether part of MS-DOS should be loaded into the high memory area (**HMA**). To enable this feature, add this line to your **CONFIG.SYS** file:

```
dos=high
```

- It lets you use the **DeviceHigh** and **LoadHigh** commands to load **device drivers** and programs into upper memory blocks (**UMBs**). To enable this feature, add this line to your CONFIG.SYS file:

```
dos=umb
```

To enable both features, you can combine these two statements into one, like this:

```
dos=high, umb
```

The DOS command can be used only in CONFIG.SYS. For this command to work, your CONFIG.SYS must also contain a **Device** command that loads **HIMEM.SYS**. And to use the UMB feature, CONFIG.SYS must also contain a Device command that loads **EMM386.EXE**.

Doskey   With the Doskey command, you can reduce the number of keystrokes needed to use MS-DOS commands. Doskey helps in two ways:

- It maintains a "command history," a list of all the commands that you have entered at the command prompt. You can selectively recall previously entered commands and re-enter them as is or edit them first.

- It can store macros. A macro is a keystroke sequence (usually one or more MS-DOS commands) that you define and that you can use simply by typing its name at the command prompt. This lets you define your own custom commands.

To enable these features, start the Doskey program by typing *doskey* at the command prompt.

Recalling a Command

You can step back through each of the commands you have entered (most recent command first) by pressing the Up direction key. When you see the command you want to reuse, simply press Enter. (If you go too far, press the Down direction key.)

```
C:\WINDOWS>
1: cls
2: dir /oen /p
3: copy *.bmp b:\
4: del *.bmp /p
5: edit autoexec.bat
6: cd \wp
7: dir /w
8: cls
9: tree /p
10: tree /?
11: tree | more
12: word
13: doskey /m
14: type \dump.bat
15: cls
C:\WINDOWS>Line number:
```

1 To see a list of all the recent commands currently stored in memory, press F7. You can then recall a command by the number that Doskey assigns to each command.

2 Press F9, and Doskey asks for the line number of the command you want to recall.

3 Type the number and press Enter, and Doskey displays the associated command at the command prompt—ready for you to re-enter or edit.

Editing the Command Line

Sometimes you'll want to enter a command that's almost the same as one you've previously entered. No problem! After Doskey displays a command at the command prompt, you can use the Left and Right direction keys to move the cursor within the command. Then type the characters that you want to change. (By default, each character you type replaces a character in the displayed command; if you want to insert additional characters before the cursor, press the Ins key before you type.) To delete a character from the displayed command, move the cursor to the character and press Del. When the command looks the way you want it, press Enter. (You don't need to move the cursor to the end of the line before you press Enter.)

Doskey also recognizes other keys for quickly moving the cursor and for selectively copying or deleting parts of a previously entered command. For a complete list, see "Command Line Editing Keys" in the Quick Reference section.

continues

Doskey *(continued)*

Creating a Macro

You create a macro with a Doskey command that includes the name you want to assign to the macro as well as the macro text itself, like this:

```
doskey ro=attrib +r *.*
```

This macro uses the **Attrib** command to set the read-only **file attribute** for all files in the **current directory**. The name of the macro is ro.

The easiest way to create a group of macros that you use repeatedly is to add the Doskey macro-definition lines to your **AUTOEXEC.BAT** file or another **batch program**.

Using a Macro

To use a macro, you simply enter its name at the command prompt—just as you would use any MS-DOS command. To use the preceding example macro, type *ro* and press Enter.

To see a list of all the macros currently in memory, type *doskey /m.*

Getting Fancy with Macros

A macro can contain more than a single, simple command. Special characters in macros let you create macros with multiple commands, **redirection** and **piping** symbols, and replaceable **parameters**. You can use these special characters in a macro definition:

$T	Separates commands; equivalent to pressing Enter
$G	Represents the > redirection symbol
$L	Represents the < redirection symbol
$B	Represents the ¦ pipe symbol
$1–$9	Replaceable parameters; when you use a macro, Doskey substitutes the first word after the macro name on the command line for $1, the second word for $2, and so on
$*	Replaceable parameter; when you use a macro, Doskey substitutes all information after the macro name for $*
$$	Represents the dollar sign ($)

The following example uses some of these characters.

```
doskey cdd=cd $1$tdir /w /ogn
```

The cdd macro first changes to the directory you specify and then, so you can get your bearings, displays a wide-format directory listing of that directory. To use it to change to your DOS directory, for example, type *cdd \dos*. Doskey then enters these commands:

```
cd \dos
dir /w /ogn
```

DOS Shell ❖ **MS-DOS Shell**

DoubleGuard   DoubleGuard is a safety feature that was added to **DoubleSpace** in MS-DOS version 6.2. (Use **Ver** to see which version you have.) When DoubleGuard is enabled (its default setting), DoubleSpace continuously monitors its memory to be sure that no other program has corrupted it. If DoubleGuard finds an error, it immediately halts your computer instead of writing potentially incorrect information to disk.

DoubleSpace   DoubleSpace is a program that allows you to store much more information on a disk. Don't worry: It doesn't modify your drive or try to squeeze more **bytes** onto the disk. Instead, DoubleSpace works its magic by creating a "drive within a drive." (You'd think the clever marketing folks at Microsoft would make a big hoopla about their "inner drive"—but instead they call it a **CVF**, or compressed volume file.) If you create one large CVF on a drive (the normal procedure), MS-DOS uses the drive's original drive letter to refer to the CVF, and assigns a new drive letter to refer to the original drive, which is called the *host drive*. DoubleSpace is included with MS-DOS versions 6 and later.

You can work with DoubleSpace in either of two ways: using a full-screen interface with drop-down menus and dialog boxes, or entering lengthy commands at the command prompt. Although the latter method is sometimes useful for impressing your friends with your knowledge of MS-DOS, the DoubleSpace command has dozens of command-line switches and parameters. Because DoubleSpace is something that you rarely revisit after setting it up, it's just not worth remembering all those cryptic commands. So in this section, we use the full-screen interface.

Creating a Compressed Drive

1   Use the ChkDsk /F command to be sure your hard disk doesn't have any cross-linked files or other errors, and to be sure you have enough free space to install DoubleSpace. (The "bytes available on disk" should be at least 1,200,000.)

2   Log on to the network if you use one. That way, DoubleSpace won't use any of the drive letters that you normally use for network connections.

3   At the command prompt, type *dblspace*. If you're running DoubleSpace for the first time, this command runs the DoubleSpace Setup program, which copies some files to the **root directory** of drive C and then begins to create a DoubleSpace drive. Choose Express Setup, and the Setup program automatically compresses drive C.

You can compress additional drives by running the DoubleSpace program again. Type *dblspace*, but this time you'll see the DoubleSpace program (instead of its Setup program):

To compress an existing drive, choose Existing Drive from the Compress menu, and then follow the on-screen prompts. This command converts the entire drive (except for a small area that DoubleSpace reserves for uncompressed files) to a compressed drive, compressing all the existing files as it goes.

Alternatively, you can create a new drive using only the free space on an existing drive. To do that, choose Create New Drive from the Compress menu.

continues

DoubleSpace *(continued)*

Compressing Floppy Disks

DoubleSpace can also pack more information onto **floppy disks**. You can read a DoubleSpace-compressed floppy disk on any computer—as long as it has DoubleSpace installed. To create a compressed floppy disk, follow these steps:

1 Insert a formatted floppy disk in the drive. It must have at least 650 **KB** of free space. (Use the **ChkDsk** command to be sure. To check the disk in drive A, type *chkdsk a:*.)

2 At the command prompt, type *dblspace*.

3 Choose Existing Drive from the Compress menu.

```
 Drive  Compress  Tools  Help

        Select the drive you want to compress.

                              Current        Projected
                 Drive        Free Space     Free Space

                   B           0.7 MB          2.1 MB
                   C          29.6 MB        262.0 MB




        Use the UP and DOWN ARROW keys to select the drive you want
        to compress, and then press ENTER.

        To return to the previous screen, press ESC.



 ENTER=Continue  F1=Help  ESC=Previous screen
```

4 Highlight the drive you want to compress and press Enter.

If you use the floppy disk on a computer running MS-DOS version 6.2, you simply insert the disk and use it like any other—except you have a lot more room. Version 6.0, however, doesn't have **Automount**, the feature that lets DoubleSpace instantly recognize compressed disks. To use such a disk with Version 6.0, insert the disk and then choose Mount from DoubleSpace's Drive menu, or type this command at the prompt:

```
dblspace /mount a:
```

D

Do you use compressed floppies frequently?

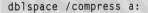

OK, OK. Here's an opportunity to show off with the DoubleSpace command-line interface: a command that's easy to remember, and one you might use frequently. Best of all, it's faster than using the full-screen interface. To compress a floppy disk in drive A, at the command prompt type:

```
dblspace /compress a:
```

Uncompressing a Compressed Drive

In the unlikely event that you change your mind, you can change a compressed drive back to a normal, uncompressed drive. This works only if all the files on the compressed drive will fit on the drive after it's uncompressed. To uncompress a drive with MS-DOS version 6.2, follow these steps:

1 At the command prompt, type *dblspace*.

2 Select the drive you want to uncompress.

3 Choose Uncompress from the Tools menu.

After you uncompress the last compressed drive on your system, DoubleSpace removes its files from the root directory, and it no longer uses disk space or memory. (The necessary files remain in your DOS directory if you decide to reuse DoubleSpace again later.)

Uncompressing with MS-DOS version 6.0

Version 6.0 doesn't include an Uncompress command, and undoing DoubleSpace is a ticklish process of moving files from the compressed drive to an uncompressed drive, resizing the compressed drive, and then moving more files. All in all, you're better off springing the $10 to upgrade to version 6.2 and then uncompressing.

continues

DoubleSpace *(continued)*

Learning More About Compressed Files

DoubleSpace can report information about the actual size of a compressed disk, the name of the CVF, and other juicy tidbits. At the main DoubleSpace screen, select a drive and then choose Info from the Drive menu.

```
┌──────────── Compressed Drive Information ────────────┐
│ Compressed drive D is stored on uncompressed drive C │
│ in the file C:\DBLSPACE.000.                         │
│                                                      │
│     Space used:            0.89 MB                   │
│     Compression ratio:     1.3 to 1                  │
│                                                      │
│     Space free:            1.06 MB                   │
│     Est. compression ratio: 2.0 to 1                 │
│     Fragmentation:         1%                        │
│                                                      │
│     Total space:           1.95 MB                   │
│                                                      │
│  «  OK  »   « Size »   « Ratio »   « Help »          │
└──────────────────────────────────────────────────────┘
```

You can get information about the compression ratio of each file on a compressed drive with the **Dir** command's /C switch. For example, at the command prompt type *dir \dos /c*.

If you use Windows, File Manager offers a nifty graph of your compressed drive. To see it, choose DoubleSpace Info from the **File Manager Tools menu**.

```
┌────────────── DoubleSpace Info ──────────────┐
│ Drive D is stored on uncompressed drive P    │
│ in the file P:\DBLSPACE.000.      ┌─ Close ─┐ │
│ ┌─Compressed Drive D─┐            └─────────┘ │
│ │ ■ Space used:    44.09 MB        ┌─ Help ─┐ │
│ │   Compression ratio: 1.4 to 1    └────────┘ │
│ │                                             │
│ │ ■ Space free:    256.10 MB                  │
│ │   Estimated compression ratio: 2.0 to 1     │
│ │                                             │
│ │ Total space:     300.20 MB    ┌Show Details┐│
└──────────────────────────────────────────────┘
```

Click the Show Details button to see compression information about each selected file.

```
┌────────────── DoubleSpace Info ──────────────┐
│ Drive D is stored on uncompressed drive P    │
│ in the file P:\DBLSPACE.000.      ┌─ Close ─┐ │
│ ┌─Compressed Drive D─┐            └─────────┘ │
│ │ ■ Space used:    44.09 MB        ┌─ Help ─┐ │
│ │   Compression ratio: 1.4 to 1    └────────┘ │
│ │                                             │
│ │ ■ Space free:    256.10 MB                  │
│ │   Estimated compression ratio: 2.0 to 1     │
│ │                                             │
│ │ Total space:     300.20 MB    ┌Hide Details┐│
│ Selected Files:                              │
│ LOTUS123.CHU      102912    1.8 to 1         │
│ TXTWLYT.CHU       223552    1.9 to 1         │
│ GRAM.DLL          375808    1.6 to 1         │
│ HYPH.DLL           21680    1.6 to 1         │
│ WORDHELP.DLL       19456    2.4 to 1         │
│ WORDRES.DLL        69120    2.8 to 1         │
│ File location:   D:\WINWORD6                 │
│ Compression ratio for the selected files: 1.3 to 1 │
└──────────────────────────────────────────────┘
```

Defragmenting a Compressed Drive

You'll find a Defragment command on DoubleSpace's Tools menu. But unlike the MS-DOS **Defrag** command, the DoubleSpace Defragment command doesn't speed up your disk. Instead, it consolidates a compressed drive's free space, which allows you to reduce the size of the drive, and *might* allow you to squeeze another file or two onto the drive.

More shameless self promotion

DoubleSpace is a complex program that can't be fully explained in a few short pages. (Even the online **Help** system includes over 40 pages of information about DoubleSpace, and that doesn't include the help information built into the DoubleSpace application itself.) If you're interested in knowing more about how DoubleSpace works and how to use it most effectively (and have a few laughs along the way), take a look at *Microsoft Press Guide to DoubleSpace* by Doug Lowe (Microsoft Press, 1993).

Echo

The Echo command is used in **batch programs** to control the display of command lines. When you run a batch program, each line in the batch program is normally displayed on the screen as it executes. If you want a batch program to run "silently" (that is, without cluttering the screen with the text of the batch program itself), begin the batch program with an *echo off* line. (And you can inhibit the display of the Echo command by preceding it with an at sign (@), like this: *@echo off.*)

Echo is also useful in batch programs for displaying a message on the screen. For example, the following command displays a greeting:

```
echo Good morning!
```

If you use Echo to display instructions for using a batch program, you might want to display a blank line between two paragraphs. Adding a period to the Echo command does just that:

```
echo.
```

continues

Echo *(continued)*

An echo is faster than walking to your printer

You can use the Echo command and **redirection** to send a "message" to your printer—one that advances the paper in your printer to the top of the next form (if you use continuous paper) or prints and ejects a page (if you use a page printer, such as a laser printer). At the command prompt, type *echo ^L > prn*. But don't press the caret (^) and then L. Instead, press Ctrl+L ; MS-DOS displays it as ^L.

Editor

MS-DOS Editor is a program for creating and modifying plain text files. It will never supplant your word processor—it doesn't even have word wrap—but it's perfect for viewing, creating, printing, or editing **batch programs**, **CONFIG.SYS**, or those ReadMe files that come with nearly every program you buy.

To start Editor, type *edit* at the command prompt. Editor's opening screen offers to explain how to use the program. After you've learned how to use Editor, you can bypass the opening screen and get right to the file you want to edit by adding its name to the command line, like this:

```
edit readme.txt
```

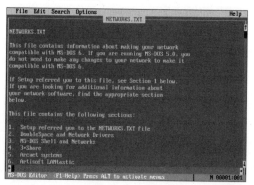

When you're through with Editor, choose Exit from the File menu to quit.

Want to see more?

The Editor screen normally displays only 21 lines at a time; you must scroll up or down to see more text. But if you add /H to the command line when you start Editor, it uses the highest resolution available for your monitor. In most cases, that means you can see nearly twice as many lines.

Edlin   What you're looking at here is a piece of history. Edlin is a line editor—word processing at its simplest. Archaeologists and computer buffs have been studying its cryptic interface for years, and only recently realized that the **Editor** program included with MS-DOS versions 5 and later is a much better way to create and modify text files.

For an up-close look at this archaic program, you need to order the **Supplemental Disk,** for Edlin is not included with MS-DOS version 6 or later.

EMM386.EXE   The EMM386.EXE **device driver** allows you to use **DeviceHigh** and **LoadHigh** commands to load other device drivers and programs into upper memory blocks (**UMBs**). Loading device drivers and programs this way leaves more conventional **memory** free for other programs. To enable this feature, your **CONFIG.SYS** file must contain these lines:

```
device=c:\dos\himem.sys
device=c:\dos\emm386.exe
dos=umb
```

The EMM386.EXE device driver also provides expanded memory to programs that require it. (Such programs include "expanded memory," "LIM-EMS," or "VCPI" in their list of system requirements; check the program's documentation.)

The EMM386.EXE device driver can be used only on computers that have a 386, 486, or Pentium processor.

EMS Memory :: **Memory**

Environment Variable

An environment variable is a piece of data that MS-DOS stores and makes available to programs—including **batch programs**—that reference it by name. For example, many programs look for an environment variable named TEMP that contains the name of a directory to use for storing temporary files.

To refer to an environment variable in a batch program, place the variable's name between two percent signs. For example, the following batch-program line uses the **CD** command to make the directory name stored in the TEMP variable the **current directory**.

```
cd %temp%
```

:: **Set**

Erase

The Erase command is exactly equivalent to the **Del** command—except it's two more keystrokes whenever you want to delete a file!

ErrorLevel

Several MS-DOS commands (and some other programs, as well) set an exit code—a special numeric variable called ErrorLevel—when they finish running. The number that the command or program assigns to the ErrorLevel variable is determined by *how* the command finished: Did it successfully complete its task? Did it find errors? Did the user stop the task before normal completion?

In a **batch program,** you can display a message or take certain action based on the ErrorLevel set by a command.

MS-DOS Commands That Produce an Exit Code

The following commands produce an exit code that you can test with If
ErrorLevel. Check online **Help** for each command to see a list of its
exit codes and their meaning.

Anti-Virus (MSAV)	**Format**
ChkDsk	Keyb
Choice	**Move**
Defrag	**Replace**
DelTree	**Restore**
DiskComp	**ScanDisk**
DiskCopy	**SetVer**
Find	**XCopy**

⁙ **If**

Exit   The Exit command closes the command processor (if
more than one is running) that was started by the **Command** command or, more likely, the MS-DOS Prompt
icon in Windows.

Expand   Most of the files on the original MS-DOS disks are
stored in a compressed format. (The compressed files are
identified by a **filename** extension that ends with an underscore.) To use one of these files, type *expand*. The Expand command asks you for the **pathname** and filename
of the file you want to expand, and then asks where you
want to put the expanded file.

Expanded Memory ⁙ **Memory**

Extended Memory ⁙ **Memory**

FastHelp   The FastHelp command shows abbreviated help information about all the MS-DOS commands. To use it, simply type *fasthelp* at the command prompt; a list of commands with a one-line summary of their function appears. For more detailed information about a particular command, add the command name to the FastHelp command line. For example, type *fasthelp copy* for more information about the Copy command. (You get the same information by typing *copy /?*.)

.·. **Help**

FastOpen   FastOpen is a **memory-resident program** that can improve the speed at which your system accesses frequently used files. It does this by caching (storing) the name and location of the most recently used files in memory; if you subsequently open one of those files again, MS-DOS can find the file's location in memory instead of searching through the disk's directory. FastOpen is most effective on disks with large directories. You can start FastOpen from the command prompt by appending the letter of the drive(s) you want FastOpen to cache. For example, to cache drives C and D, type this:

```
fastopen c: d:
```

A better way to start FastOpen

If you decide you want to use FastOpen, instead of starting it from the command prompt or from **AUTOEXEC.BAT**, you can use the **Install** command to add it to your **CONFIG.SYS** file, like this:

```
install=c:\dos\fastopen.exe c:
```

FC

The FC (File Compare) command compares two files and displays the differences between them. FC is most effective with unformatted text files, such as **batch programs** and the like. To compare two files, you specify the names of the files, like this:

```
fc \autoexec.bat \dos\autoexec.umb
```

FC compares the files line by line. When it encounters a difference between the files, it displays the name of each file, the different lines, and the lines before and after the section that differs.

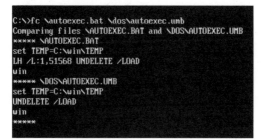

```
C:\>fc \autoexec.bat \dos\autoexec.umb
Comparing files \AUTOEXEC.BAT and \DOS\AUTOEXEC.UMB
***** \AUTOEXEC.BAT
set TEMP=C:\win\TEMP
LH /L:1,51568 UNDELETE /LOAD
win
***** \DOS\AUTOEXEC.UMB
set TEMP=C:\win\TEMP
UNDELETE /LOAD
win
*****
```

File   The information you store on a disk—such as a document or spreadsheet—is saved in a file. Each file is given a
name and is stored in a **directory**. Programs—and even
MS-DOS itself—are also stored in files. Because the file is
the basic unit of disk storage, MS-DOS has many commands for managing files:

Attributes—**Attrib; File Attributes**

Comparing—**FC; DiskComp**

Copying—**Copy; XCopy; Backup; Replace; Restore; DiskCopy**

Creating, changing—**Editor**

Listing, finding—**Dir**

Moving—**Move**

Naming—**Filename; File Specification; Ren**

Printing—**Print**

Removing—**Del; DelTree; Format**

Restoring—**Undelete; Unformat; Backup; Restore**

Uncompressing—**Expand**

Viewing—**Editor; Type; More**

FILE0000.CHK   When they find and fix errors in a disk's directory structure, the **ChkDsk** and **ScanDisk** commands as-
semble the stranded file fragments in files with names like
FILE0000.CHK. You can use **Type** or **More** to view these
files (and use **Editor** or your word processor to save any
snippets of text that seem useful), but in most cases, they
contain only cryptic codes and beeps that can't be used
for anything except making wacky displays on your
screen. Put them out of your misery: Type *del *.chk.*

File Attributes   File attributes are indicator flags that MS-DOS stores as part of the directory information about each file. MS-DOS maintains four such attributes for each file: archive, system, hidden, and read-only.

- The archive attribute tracks whether a file has been backed up since it was last modified. When a file is created or changed, the archive attribute is set—meaning the file needs to be backed up. When you back up the file with **Backup** or **XCopy**, MS-DOS clears the archive attribute. Modifying the file resets the archive attribute.

- The system attribute identifies operating system files, and is typically used in combination with the hidden attribute.

- The hidden attribute is used to "hide" files so that, by default, they don't appear in **Dir** listings and they aren't affected by other MS-DOS commands such as **Del** and **Copy**. It's typically used in combination with the system attribute.

- The read-only attribute is used to protect files from changes. When a file has the read-only attribute set, you cannot delete the file or modify its contents.

Use at your own risk

Don't rely on the file attributes to afford total protection for your important files. Many programs can overlook these attributes and, for example, delete a file that has system, hidden, and read-only attributes set. Even some MS-DOS commands can change a file without changing its attributes. **Ren**, for example, renames a file, regardless of its attributes. And the **Move** command can move a read-only file to another disk—effectively deleting it from its original location.

Viewing and changing attributes—**Attrib**

Limiting directory display to files with certain attributes—**Dir**

Using attributes to control backup behavior—**Backup; XCopy**

Protecting files on floppy disks—**Floppy Disk**

File Manager Tools Menu

When you install MS-DOS version 6 on a computer that already has Microsoft Windows installed, the Setup program adds a new menu to File Manager in Windows. The Tools menu includes three commands:

• The Backup command starts **Backup** for Windows.

• The Antivirus command starts **Anti-Virus** for Windows.

• The DoubleSpace Info command displays compression information about a **DoubleSpace**-compressed drive and the files on that drive.

In addition, Setup adds a new command to File Manager's File menu: The Undelete command starts **Undelete** for Windows.

If you use Windows for Workgroups, you'll see that the File Manager toolbar includes buttons for each of these commands.

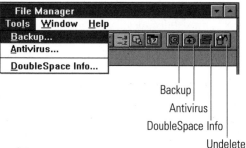

Backup
Antivirus
DoubleSpace Info
Undelete

Installing Windows after you install MS-DOS

If you install Microsoft Windows after you install MS-DOS (or you chose not to install the Windows-based utilities when you installed MS-DOS), your File Manager won't have these additional commands and buttons. To add them, exit Windows, insert disk 1 of your original MS-DOS version 6 disks into your floppy drive, and type *a:setup /e*. The MS-DOS Setup program installs the Windows-based versions of Anti-Virus, Backup, and Undelete, updates File Manager, and adds a **Microsoft Tools program group** to Program Manager.

Filename   Just like people, each file on a disk must have a name. The rules for naming files are a little more restrictive than people-naming rules. (Are there any?)

- Length: A filename can be from one through eight characters long, plus it may have an extension up to three characters in length. A period separates the extension from the first part of the filename.

- Characters: A filename (including the extension) can include letters of the alphabet (MS-DOS makes no distinction between uppercase and lowercase letters), numbers, and most other characters on your keyboard. But it can't include a space or any of the following:

  " * + , . / : ; < = > ? [\ ] |

- Uniqueness: Just as each person in a family has a unique name (or at least a "Jr." or identifying number at the end of the name), every file in a **directory** must have a unique name. (But you can have identically named files in different directories.)

  File Specification; Pathname

Files   The Files command specifies the number of files that MS-DOS can have open at one time. The default value is 8, but that's rarely enough for today's resource-hungry programs. Although you might use only one document at a time, some programs need access to many program files. Start with 20 or 30 files; if that's not enough, you'll see a "Not enough file handles" (or similar) error.

The Files command can be used only in **CONFIG.SYS**. To set the number of files to 20, include this line in your CONFIG.SYS file:

```
files=20
```

File Specification   Many MS-DOS commands and other programs ask you to furnish a file specification—sometimes
abbreviated as *filespec*—which is a description of how to
find a file. A complete file specification includes the letter
of the drive that contains the file and a colon, the path to
the file's **directory**, and the name of the file, including its
extension. Like this, for example:

```
c:\dos\format.com
```

Drive
letter

Pathname

Filename

You can omit the drive specification when you refer to a
file on the **current drive**, and you can omit the directory
path when you refer to a file in the **current directory**.

Some MS-DOS commands and other programs let you
refer to a group of files by using **wildcard** characters in a
file specification. For example, to specify all files that have
a COM extension in the DOS directory, use this file
specification:

```
c:\dos\*.com
```

❖ . and ..

Filter   A filter is a command that takes input from a file or another command, and then produces output that meets
the filter criteria. MS-DOS includes two such commands:
Find and **Sort**.

The Find command allows only lines that contain a text
string you specify to pass through the filter.

The Sort command arranges lines of text from an input file
or another command in alphabetical order and then
displays them on the screen or saves them to an output file.

❖ **Piping; Redirection**

Find

The Find command is a filter that scans a text file (or the output of another command) for the occurrence of a text string you specify, and then displays the lines that contain the text string (or saves them to a file).

Finding Text in a File

In its simplest form, you tell Find the text you want to search for and the name of the file to search, like this:

```
find "LANtastic" c:\dos\networks.txt
```

This command searches NETWORKS.TXT for any occurrence of "LANtastic" (note that Find's search is case sensitive, so the text must match uppercase and lowercase letters exactly) and then displays the lines that contain "LANtastic" on the screen, like this:

```
C:\DOS>find "LANtastic" networks.txt

---------- NETWORKS.TXT
6.  Artisoft LANtastic
6.  Artisoft LANtastic
If you are using any version of Artisoft LANtastic,
shut down the LANtastic server before you run MS-DOS 6
Artisoft LANtastic versions 3.02 and higher are compatible
If you are using a LANtastic version earlier than 2.5,
If you are using LANtastic versions 2.5 through 3.01,
To update LANtastic versions 2.5 through 3.01:
1.  Shut down the LANtastic server. You can leave the
defaults for the LANtastic 2Mbps adapter, include the
LANtastic network software if the server service is loaded.
compatible with LANtastic network software.
NOTE  You cannot use DoubleSpace to compress a drive on a LANtastic server
```

Although this command shows each line that contains the text you're looking for, it doesn't tell you where that text occurs in the file. For that information, add the /N switch, which places a line number before each line. (You can use that information to find the text with a program like MS-DOS Editor, for example, which displays the cursor's line number in the lower right corner of the screen, as shown on the next page.)

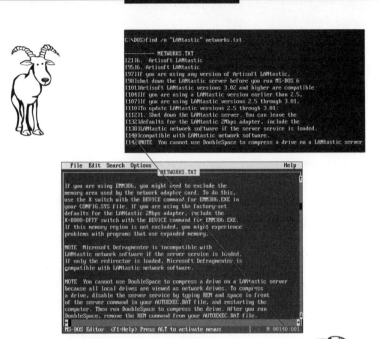

```
C:\DOS>find /n "LANtastic" networks.txt

---------- NETWORKS.TXT
[216]. Artisoft LANtastic
[95]6. Artisoft LANtastic
[97]If you are using any version of Artisoft LANtastic,
[98]shut down the LANtastic server before you run MS-DOS 6
[101]Artisoft LANtastic versions 3.02 and higher are compatible
[104]If you are using a LANtastic version earlier than 2.5,
[107]If you are using LANtastic versions 2.5 through 3.01,
[110]To update LANtastic versions 2.5 through 3.01:
[112]31. Shut down the LANtastic server. You can leave the
[132]defaults for the LANtastic 2Mbps adapter, include the
[138]LANtastic network software if the server service is loaded.
[140]compatible with LANtastic network software.
[142]NOTE You cannot use DoubleSpace to compress a drive on a LANtastic server
```

```
 File  Edit  Search  Options                                       Help
                              NETWORKS.TXT
 If you are using EMM386, you might need to exclude the
 memory area used by the network adapter card. To do this,
 use the X switch with the DEVICE command for EMM386.EXE in
 your CONFIG.SYS file. If you are using the factory-set
 defaults for the LANtastic 2Mbps adapter, include the
 X=D000-DFFF switch with the DEVICE command for EMM386.EXE.
 If this memory region is not excluded, you might experience
 problems with programs that use expanded memory.

 NOTE  Microsoft Defragmenter is incompatible with
 LANtastic network software if the server service is loaded.
 If only the redirector is loaded, Microsoft Defragmenter is
 compatible with LANtastic network software.

 NOTE  You cannot use DoubleSpace to compress a drive on a LANtastic server
 because all local drives are viewed as network drives. To compress
 a drive, disable the server service by typing REM and space in front
 of the server command in your AUTOEXEC.BAT file, and restarting the
 computer. Then run DoubleSpace to compress the drive. After you run
 DoubleSpace, remove the REM command from your AUTOEXEC.BAT file.
 MS-DOS Editor  <F1=Help> Press ALT to activate menus          N 00140:001
```

Searching in more than one file

Unlike many MS-DOS commands, you cannot use **wildcard** characters to specify more than one file on the Find command line. Here's an application for the **For** command. In the following example, the For command causes the Find command to run once for each TXT file, which has the same effect as using a wildcard with Find:

```
for %a in (*.txt) do find "LANtastic" %a
```

Floppy Disk

A floppy disk stores files and directories—exactly like a hard disk. But there are a few differences:

- Floppy disks can be removed from the computer, which makes them useful for moving information between computers and for archival storage.

- Floppy disks cannot hold as much information as a hard disk.

- Floppy disks are not as fast as hard disks for accessing information.

Before you use a floppy disk, it must be formatted—a process that prepares a disk for use by erasing all data on the disk and creating an empty **root directory**.

Protecting Files on Floppy Disks

Floppy drives have a feature that allows you to protect a disk from changes. Files on "write-protected" disks cannot be altered or deleted, nor can files be added.

To write-protect a 3½" disk, slide the small plastic tab on the back of the disk so that the window in the upper right corner is open.

To write-protect a 5¼" disk, cover the notch in the upper right corner of the disk with a self-adhesive sticker. A sheet of these "write-protect tabs" is usually furnished with each box of disks.

Comparing disks—**DiskComp**

Compressing a disk—**DoubleSpace**

Copying a disk—**DiskCopy**

Formatting a disk—**Format**

Using floppy disks to move information

Do you use floppy disks for moving information from one computer to another? You might find it more convenient to connect the two computers and use **Interlnk**.

Floppy Drive   Almost all personal computers have at least one floppy drive, a **disk drive** for removable **floppy disks**. MS-DOS supports the following types of floppy drives:

Disk size and type	Capacity
3½" extra-high density	2.88 MB
3½" high density	1.44 MB
3½" low density	720 KB
5¼" high density	1.2 MB
5¼" low density	360 KB

For   The For command lets you execute an MS-DOS command repeatedly—once for each element in a set. For is one of the most convoluted commands in the MS-DOS arsenal, but it's worth knowing. The For command includes a couple of unusual components:

- A *variable*, which is a single character (any character except the numerals 0 through 9) that follows a percent sign (%).

- A *set*, which can be one or more **filenames** (you can use **wildcard** characters in the **file specification**) or text strings. The set must be enclosed in parentheses.

- A *command*, which can be any valid MS-DOS command.

For each element in the set, MS-DOS replaces the variable name with the set element and then executes the command. Consider the following example:

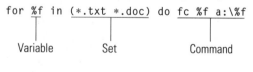

```
for %f in (*.txt *.doc) do fc %f a:\%f
```
     Variable   Set   Command

This command uses the **FC** command to compare the contents of each file with a TXT or DOC extension in the **current directory** with a like-named file on the disk in drive A. Suppose the current directory contains the following files:

NETWORKS.TXT
OLDSOCKS.DOC
OS2.TXT
README.TXT
TIME2GO.DOC

Entering the For command shown above has the effect of entering the following sequence of commands:

```
fc networks.txt a:\networks.txt
fc os2.txt a:\os2.txt
fc readme.txt a:\readme.txt
fc oldsocks.doc a:\oldsocks.doc
fc time2go.doc a:\time2go.doc
```

Using the For command in a batch program

You can use the For command at the command prompt or in a **batch program**—but there's one difference. At the command prompt, you use a single percent sign before the variable; in a batch program, you must use *two* percent signs. Our example above, then, looks like this when used in a batch program:

```
for %%f in (*.txt *.doc) do fc %%f a:\%%f
```

Format

The Format command prepares a disk for use with MS-DOS by erasing all data from the disk, checking the disk for damaged areas, and creating a new **root directory**.

Formatting a Disk—The Fast and Easy Way

To format a disk, you add the letter of the drive that contains the disk to the Format command. But you can speed up the Format command by adding the /Q (for "quick") switch. Take the following steps to format the **floppy disk** in drive A using the quick method. (If the disk hasn't been previously formatted, Format automatically reverts to its standard method of scanning the entire disk for damaged areas.)

1 At the command prompt, type *format a: /q* and press Enter. MS-DOS responds:

```
Insert new diskette for drive A:
and press ENTER when ready...
```

2 Insert a blank disk in drive A and press Enter. Format begins its work and then pauses to ask:

```
Checking existing disk format.
Saving UNFORMAT information.
QuickFormatting 720K
Format complete.

Volume label (11 characters, ENTER for none)?
```

3 If you want the disk to have a **volume label**, type it and press Enter. If not, simply press Enter. Format then completes its mission and reports:

```
    730,112 bytes total disk space
    730,112 bytes available on disk

      1,024 bytes in each allocation unit.
        713 allocation units available on disk.

Volume Serial Number is 0724-14F9

QuickFormat another (Y/N)?
```

4 When it finishes, the Format command asks if you want to format another disk. If you do, type *Y* (yes) and press Enter; then go to step 2. If you don't want to format another disk, type *N* (no) and press Enter; the command prompt returns.

Making a system disk

You can use the Format command to create a bootable disk, which allows you to **boot** your system from a floppy disk. When you add the /S switch to the Format command line, Format copies COMMAND.COM, MSDOS.SYS, and IO.SYS to the new disk. (The latter two files have the hidden **file attribute**, so they won't appear in a **Dir** listing.)

Adding a volume label after formatting—**Vol**

Adding system files after formatting—**Sys**

Undoing the effects of Format—**Unformat**

GoTo   The GoTo command is used in **batch programs** to go to a specific line in the program. You follow the GoTo command with a label that identifies the program line you want to execute next. For example, when MS-DOS encounters this line in a batch program:

```
goto help1
```

MS-DOS reads the batch program from the beginning, looking for a line that looks like this:

```
:help1
```

MS-DOS then continues executing the batch program with the line that follows the "help1" label. A colon must precede each label. A label cannot contain spaces, and MS-DOS uses only the first eight characters of each label.

continues

GoTo *(continued)*

Branching based on your configuration

You can use the contents of an **environment variable** as a destination for a GoTo command; to do so, you put a percent sign on each side of the environment variable name. This ability is especially useful if you use **multiple configurations** in your **CONFIG.SYS** file. When you do, MS-DOS creates a CONFIG environment variable that contains the name of the configuration block you select at startup.

You can then branch to different parts of your batch program by including a line like this:

```
goto %config%
```

Then create labels in your batch program that match the configuration-block names from CONFIG.SYS. This technique is commonly used in **AUTOEXEC.BAT**.

 Choice; ErrorLevel; If

Graphics

Graphics is a **memory-resident program** that lets you print any graphical image displayed on your screen. The Graphics program supports a variety of popular IBM and Hewlett-Packard printers.

Most graphics programs provide printer support that lets you print images you create with that program. The only time you need the Graphics program is when you want to print a "screen dump"—a printed copy of the image on your screen—of a graphics screen.

Loading the Graphics Program

To load the Graphics program from a **batch program** or the command prompt, simply type *graphics* followed by the name of your printer. For example:

```
graphics laserjet
```

See the online **Help** for a complete list of printers supported by Graphics.

Printing a Graphical Image

1 Load the Graphics program as described above.

2 Display the image you want to print.

3 Press Shift+PrtSc. (Hold down the Shift key and press PrtSc.)

Hard Disk ⁖ Disk Drive

Help

When you're stuck in the jungle and you can't find your MS-DOS manual, don't worry. MS-DOS offers online help for all its commands. ("Online" is how software publishers euphemistically describe the computer-based documentation that has replaced the heavy paper manuals of yore. Be thankful for all the trees—and spotted owls—that have been saved by this trend.)

Getting Help on a Command

When you just need a quick reminder about a command's purpose or syntax, add /? to the end of the command line before you press Enter. MS-DOS displays a brief description of the command and lists all the command-line switches for that command. For example, if you type *find /?*, you'll see this:

```
C:\>find /?
Searches for a text string in a file or files.

FIND [/V] [/C] [/N] [/I] "string" [[drive:][path]filename[ ...]]

  /V        Displays all lines NOT containing the specified string.
  /C        Displays only the count of lines containing the string.
  /N        Displays line numbers with the displayed lines.
  /I        Ignores the case of characters when searching for the string.
  "string"  Specifies the text string to find.
  [drive:][path]filename
            Specifies a file or files to search.

If a pathname is not specified, FIND searches the text typed at the prompt
or piped from another command.
```

continues

Help *(continued)*

Understanding the command syntax

Help for each command includes a "syntax" section, which shows exactly how to type the command. But the format of the syntax section itself is somewhat cryptic. Here's what it means:

- Text shown in uppercase letters must be typed exactly as shown. You should also include spaces where they appear.

- Text shown in lowercase letters must be replaced with appropriate text. For example, type *c:* in place of "drive:".

- Text enclosed in square brackets is optional. Don't include the brackets if you want to include the option.

- Text separated by a pipe symbol (|) represents a choice; you must select only one option.

- An ellipsis (...) indicates that you can repeat the parameter that precedes it (if you want to specify more than one filename, for example).

When You Can't Remember the Name of a Command

To see a list of all the MS-DOS commands and a brief description of their function, type *fasthelp*. MS-DOS displays a list like the following, pausing after each screenful:

```
For more information on a specific command, type FASTHELP command-name.
APPEND    Allows programs to open data files in specified directories as if
          they were in the current directory.
ATTRIB    Displays or changes file attributes.
BREAK     Sets or clears extended CTRL+C checking.
CD        Displays the name of or changes the current directory.
CHCP      Displays or sets the active code page number.
CHDIR     Displays the name of or changes the current directory.
CHKDSK    Checks a disk and displays a status report.
CLS       Clears the screen.
COMMAND   Starts a new instance of the MS-DOS command interpreter.
COMP      Compares the contents of two files or sets of files.
COPY      Copies one or more files to another location.
CTTY      Changes the terminal device used to control your system.
DATE      Displays or sets the date.
DBLSPACE  Sets up or configures DoubleSpace compressed drives.
DEBUG     Starts Debug, a program testing and editing tool.
DEFRAG    Reorganizes the files on a disk to optimize the disk.
DEL       Deletes one or more files.
DELOLDOS  Deletes the OLD_DOS.1 directory and the files it contains.
DELTREE   Deletes a directory and all the files and subdirectories in it.
DIR       Displays a list of files and subdirectories in a directory.
DISKCOMP  Compares the contents of two floppy disks.
---More---
```

Getting Detailed Help

The most detailed and comprehensive help for MS-DOS commands is obtained by typing *help*. This command starts MS-DOS Help, a full-screen application.

```
 File  Search                                          Help
              ┌─────MS-DOS Help: Command Reference─────┐
                                                           ↑
Use the scroll bars to see more commands. Or, press the PAGE DOWN key. For
more information about using MS-DOS Help, choose How to Use MS-DOS Help
from the Help menu, or press F1. To exit MS-DOS Help, press ALT, F, X.

<What's New in MS-DOS 6.2?>

<ANSI.SYS>               <Erase>                <Nlsfunc>
<Append>                 <Exit>                 <Numlock>
<Attrib>                 <Expand>               <Path>
<Batch commands>         <Fasthelp>             <Pause>
<Break>                  <Fastopen>             <Power>
<Buffers>                <Fc>                   <POWER.EXE>
<Call>                   <Fcbs>                 <Print>
<Cd>                     <Fdisk>                <Prompt>
<Chcp>                   <Files>                <Qbasic>
<Chdir>                  <Find>                 <RAMDRIVE.SYS>
<Chkdsk>                 <For>                  <Rd>
<CHKSTATE.SYS>           <Format>               <Rem>
<Choice>                 <Goto>                 <Ren>
<Cls>                    <Graphics>             <Rename>
<Command>                <Help>                 <Replace>
<Alt+C=Contents> <Alt+N=Next> <Alt+B=Back>          N 00006:002
```

Bright green brackets surround the names of topics in the help system that you can view.

• To go to a topic, click its name with the mouse or move the cursor to the name and then press Enter.

• Press Tab to move the cursor to the next topic name.

• Press Shift+Tab to move to the previous name.

• Pressing a letter key moves the cursor to the next topic name that starts with that letter.

• Press Alt+C to return to the Help Contents screen.

• Press Alt+B to step back through the topics you've already viewed.

• If you want to browse through the help "manual," press Alt+N to view the next topic.

To quit the Help program, choose the Exit command from the File menu. (Press Alt+F and then press X.)

continues

Help *(continued)*

Going Directly to a Topic

To bypass the Contents screen and go directly to the detailed help
screen for a command, add the name of the command to the command
line when you start Help. For example, to view help for the ScanDisk
command, type *help scandisk*.

Try F1 first

Although it doesn't work at the command prompt, the F1 key is be-
coming a standard method for summoning help within an application. It does so in
each of the full-screen applications included with MS-DOS, such as **Anti-Virus**,
Backup, **Editor**, and even the MS-DOS Help application itself.

Printing a Help Topic

Sometimes pixels on a computer screen are inadequate; nothing but
black ink on white paper will do. To print a topic from the Help
application, follow these steps:

1   Start Help and display the topic you want to print.

2   Choose Print from the File menu.

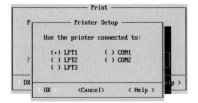

3   If your printer is attached to the LPT1 parallel port, skip to step 5. If
your printer is attached to a different port, choose Printer Setup.

4   Select the port that your printer is connected to and choose OK.

5   Choose OK in the Print dialog box.

Hidden File Attribute ⁂ Attrib; File Attributes

HIMEM.SYS HIMEM.SYS is a **device driver** that manages extended **memory**. Its purpose is to coordinate the use of extended memory (including the high memory area, or HMA) so that no two programs use the same memory at the same time.

You install HIMEM.SYS with a **Device** command in your **CONFIG.SYS** file. You must load HIMEM.SYS before you load any programs or device drivers that use extended memory. This means that HIMEM.SYS must be loaded before you can load **EMM386.EXE**, for example, as well as any device driver or program you load with **DeviceHigh** or **LoadHigh** commands. HIMEM.SYS is also required if you want to load MS-DOS into the high memory area with the **DOS** command.

To use HIMEM.SYS, make this the first line in your CONFIG.SYS file:

```
device=c:\dos\himem.sys
```

HMA HMA stands for "High Memory Area," which is the first 64 **KB** of extended **memory**.

If

The If command is used in **batch programs** to execute a command only if a certain condition is met. The If command can check for three different types of conditions:

- If can compare two text strings and execute a command if the strings are identical. (A "text string" is just a sequence of characters—not necessarily words or even letters.)

- If can check for the existence of a file you specify, and execute a command if the file exists.

- If can check the **ErrorLevel,** or exit code, from the preceding command, and execute a command if it is equal to or greater than a number you specify.

You can also instruct If to execute a command if any of these conditions is *not* true (for example, if the text strings are different, or if a file does not exist).

Comparing Text Strings

In a batch program, you sometimes want certain commands to execute depending upon the value of an **environment variable** or a command-line **parameter**. Consider this example from a batch program called FMT.BAT:

```
if "%1"=="a" goto format_a
```

If you start the batch program by typing *fmt a* at the command prompt, when this command is executed, the If command compares the first replaceable parameter (%1) with "a" and sees that they're equivalent, so it executes the *goto format_a* command. If you had instead typed *fmt b* (or *fmt A*; this text comparison is case sensitive), the If command would see that the parameter is not the same as "a," and the batch program would continue to the next line.

To execute a condition if the two strings are different, add *not* to the If command, like this:

```
if not "%config%"=="net" goto load_net
```

You can quote me on that

When you compare text strings in an If command, it's not necessary to surround the text strings with quotation marks. In fact, If compares *everything* on the two sides of the equal signs, and the quotation marks become part of the strings being compared. It's a good idea to include them, however, because if one of the strings is empty (for example, if you don't include a parameter on the command line when you start the batch program, %1 is nothing), the If command generates an error.

Checking for the Existence of a File

Sometimes you'll want a batch program to take certain action if a particular file already exists (or doesn't exist). For example:

```
if exist readme.txt type readme.txt
```

or

```
if not exist readme.txt copy %1:readme.txt
```

In both examples, the If command looks in the **current directory** for a file named README.TXT. In the first example, if the file exists, If displays the file with a **Type** command. In the second example, if the file does *not* exist, If uses the **Copy** command to copy the file to the current directory.

Using ErrorLevel

Many commands and programs set an ErrorLevel when they finish; the ErrorLevel can indicate a completion status, or it can indicate a user action such as a menu selection.

The If ErrorLevel command executes a command if the value of ErrorLevel is equal to or greater than a number you specify. If ErrorLevel is less than the specified number, batch program execution continues with the next line. Therefore, if you want to take action based on several different possible ErrorLevel values, it's important that you check for them in *descending order*, like this:

```
choice /c:ynq Yes, No, or Quit
if errorlevel 3 goto quit
if errorlevel 2 goto no
:yes
```

continues

If *(continued)*

In this example, the **Choice** command returns an ErrorLevel of 1, 2, or 3, depending on whether the user presses Y, N, or Q. If the user presses Q, the first If command is true, and the *goto quit* command is executed. If not, the next If command is executed. Note that you don't need an If statement to check for the last possible ErrorLevel setting; if none of the preceding If statements are true, then the batch program reaches that point anyway.

Include

The Include command is used in a **CONFIG.SYS** file that uses **multiple configurations.** It lets you include all the commands from one configuration block in another configuration block so that you don't have to repeat them.

Install

The Install command loads a **memory-resident program.** It can be used only in a **CONFIG.SYS** file. Loading a program with Install instead of loading the program from **AUTOEXEC.BAT** uses slightly less **memory,** but some programs won't work properly. Try it; if the program doesn't work, remove the Install command from CONFIG.SYS and add the program's startup command to AUTOEXEC.BAT.

The Install command includes the **file specification** for the program you want to load, along with any **parameters** for the program. For example, to start the **Share** program, include this line in CONFIG.SYS:

```
install=c:\dos\share.exe /l:100
```

InterInk   Interlnk is a program that lets you connect two computers so that you can access both computer's disk drives, files, and printers from a single computer. With Interlnk, you can easily copy files between computers without a fancy network.

To use Interlnk, you need either a free serial port on both computers or a free parallel port on both computers, and an appropriate cable to connect the two.

One computer is called the server; its drives and printers are available from either computer. The other computer is called the client. The client is the computer that you use to access both computers.

Setting Up Interlnk

Before you can use Interlnk, you must modify the **CONFIG.SYS** file on the client. You don't need to make any changes to the server.

1 Use **Editor** to open CONFIG.SYS.

2 Add this line:

```
device=c:\dos\interlnk.exe
```

3 Save the CONFIG.SYS file and quit Editor.

4 Press **Ctrl+Alt+Del** to restart your computer.

If the server has more than three drives

By default, Interlnk lets you access the first three drives on the server. If the server has more than three drives that you want to access, add a /DRIVES switch, like this:

```
device=c:\dos\interlnk.exe /drives:10
```

Be sure that the client's **LastDrive** setting is high enough to provide letters for all the drives.

continues

InterInk *(continued)*

Starting InterInk

On the server, type *intersvr* at the command prompt. The **Intersvr** program displays a list of all the drives and printers on the server, as shown below.

This letter indicates the server drive.

To access this server drive, use this letter on the client.

```
                    Microsoft Interlnk Server Version 1.10


    This Computer   Other Computer      This Computer   Other Computer
      (Server)        (Client)            (Server)        (Client)

   A:           equals  E:           K: (499Kb)  equals  Not Connected
   B:           equals  F:           L:          equals  Not Connected
   C: (244Mb)   equals  G:           M:          equals  Not Connected
 * D: (334Mb)   equals  H:           N:          equals  Not Connected
   E: (499Kb)   equals  I:           O:          equals  Not Connected
   F: (499Kb)   equals  J:           P: (169Mb)  equals  Not Connected
   G: (499Kb)   equals  K:           LPT1:       equals  LPT2:
   H: (499Kb)   equals  L:           LPT2:       equals  LPT3:
   I: (499Kb)   equals  Not Connected LPT3:      equals  Not Connected
   J: (499Kb)   equals  Not Connected



 Transfer: Reading   |   Port=COM1:   |   Speed=Variable   |   Alt+F4=Exit
```

The Transfer section of the status bar indicates the type of access.

An asterisk in the left margin indicates that the client is currently accessing a resource.

Accessing Server Drives and Printers

You access server drives from the client by using the drive letter shown in the Intersvr display. Using the screen shown above for example, you access the server's drive C by referring to it as drive G on the client. It works exactly like an internal drive in every respect, except it's a bit slower.

Similarly, you access a server's printers by directing your printed output to the printer port shown in the Intersvr display.

You can get a similar "cross-reference" list at the client by typing *interlnk*. A screen like the one shown below appears.

```
C:\>interlnk

    Port=COM1

    This Computer        Other Computer
       (Client)             (Server)

     E:    equals     A:
     F:    equals     B:
     G:    equals     C: (244Mb) CHINQUAPIN
     H:    equals     D: (334Mb) DELPHINIUM
     I:    equals     E: (499Mb) GLACIER
     J:    equals     F: (499Mb) GLACIER
     K:    equals     G: (499Mb) ACADIA
     L:    equals     H: (499Mb) ACADIA
     LPT2: equals     LPT1:
     LPT3: equals     LPT2:
```

Stopping the Interlnk Connection

When you are finished with Interlnk, stop the server by pressing Alt+F4 on the server's keyboard.

Intersvr   Intersvr is the program that runs on the "server" when you have two computers connected with **Interlnk.** The Intersvr program requires the server's full attention; you cannot use **Task Swapper** or Windows to switch to another application while Intersvr is running.

KB

KB is a widely used abbreviation for "kilobyte," which, as any student of Greek or the metric system can tell you, means 1000 **bytes**. Well, not quite. Because computer scientists have long been mired in the binary numbering system, a kilobyte is based on an exponential power of 2. A kilobyte is, in fact, $2 \times 2 \times 2 \times 2 \times 2 \times 2 \times 2 \times 2 \times 2 \times 2$, or 1024 bytes.

KB is commonly used to describe disk capacity, file sizes, and **memory** addresses and sizes. Be aware that, because of the 1000/1024 discrepancy, common usage is sometimes ambiguous. For example, when a program's memory requirement is specified as 430 KB, it could mean that you need 430,000 bytes of free memory to run the program—or you might need 440,320 (430 × 1024) bytes free.

 MB

Label

The Label command changes a disk's **volume label**. MS-DOS displays the volume label whenever you use the **Dir, ChkDsk,** or **Vol** command to display information about a disk.

```
B:\>dir

Volume in drive B is CS_TRANSFER ——— Volume label
Volume Serial Number is 12F2-1728
Directory of B:\
```

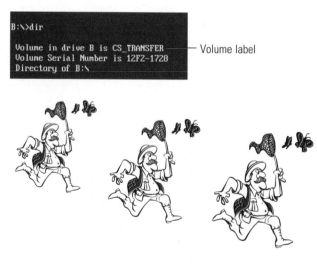

To change the volume label for the **current drive**, follow these steps:

1 At the command prompt, type *label*. MS-DOS responds:

```
Volume in drive C is CHINQUAPIN
Volume label (11 characters, ENTER for none)?
```

2 Type the new label you want and press Enter. A label can be up to 11 characters long, and it can include letters (the Label command converts lowercase letters to uppercase), numbers, spaces, and most symbols. Do not use any of the following symbols:

" & ( ) * + , . / : ; < = > ? [\ ] ^ ¦

To delete the current label, press Enter without typing a name.

If you want to leave the existing label unchanged, press **Ctrl+C** to return to the command prompt.

3 To be sure that your change took effect, you can type *vol*.

LastDrive   The LastDrive command specifies the highest drive letter you can use. Every **disk drive** in your computer — such as your **floppy drives,** hard drives, and **CD-ROM** drives—is addressed by its drive letter. You need to reserve additional drive letters if:

- You use **DoubleSpace** (Each drive that contains a compressed drive needs a drive letter to identify the host drive in addition to one for each DoubleSpace drive.)

- You use **RAMDrive** (You must reserve a drive letter for each RAM drive.)

- You set up your computer as an **Interlnk** client (You must reserve a drive letter for each drive on *both* computers.)

- You connect to a network (You must assign a drive letter to each network connection.)

- You use the **Subst** command

The LastDrive command can be used only in the **CONFIG.SYS** file. To reserve drive letters A through K (which permits access to 11 drives), for example, include this line in CONFIG.SYS:

```
lastdrive=k
```

LH LoadHigh

LoadHigh   The LoadHigh command loads a **memory-resident program** into upper **memory**, thereby retaining more conventional memory for use by other programs. (If upper memory is not available, the program loads into conventional memory.)

For the LoadHigh command to work, your computer must have extended memory (a computer with a 386, 486, or Pentium processor and more than 1 **MB** of RAM has extended memory) and the following lines must be in your **CONFIG.SYS** file.

```
device=c:\dos\himem.sys
device=c:\dos\emm386.exe
dos=umb
```

You normally use LoadHigh in **AUTOEXEC.BAT**, although you can use it in any **batch program** or at the command prompt. You simply insert *loadhigh* (or *lh*, its shortcut equivalent) at the beginning of the command to load the program. For example, to load the **Doskey** program into upper memory, use this command:

```
loadhigh doskey
```

Using LoadHigh most effectively

You can use /L and /S switches with LoadHigh to specify exactly how and where programs should load—but this fine-tuning is best done by **MemMaker**.

 DeviceHigh

MB

MB is an abbreviation for "megabyte," which means "million **bytes**." MB is commonly used to describe disk capacity, file sizes, and **memory** addresses and sizes.

Because computer scientists speak their own language, a MB is not 1,000,000 bytes, as you might expect. Instead, a MB is a "kilo kilobytes," or 1,048,576 (1024 × 1024) bytes.

KB

MD

The MD command—short for "Make Directory"—creates a new **directory**. To create a subdirectory of the **current directory**, simply append its name to the MD command, like this:

```
md homework
```

By specifying the complete path, you can create a directory that's not a subdirectory of the current directory— or even on the **current drive**. For example, to create a new directory on drive B (assuming the disk in drive B already has an ALGEBRA directory), type *md b:\algebra\homework*.

The rules for naming directories are exactly the same as those for **filenames**. By convention, however, directory names usually do not have an extension; they have only an eight-character name.

CD; RD

Mem   The Mem command displays the amount of **memory** in your computer. For each type of memory, Mem shows the total amount of memory, the amount used by programs, and the amount free for use by other programs. To use it, at the command prompt type *mem*. You'll see a report similar to this:

```
C:\>mem

Memory Type         Total  =   Used  +   Free
--------------------------------------------
Conventional         640K      44K      596K
Upper                155K     155K       0K
Reserved             384K     384K       0K
Extended (XMS)    15,205K  14,181K    1,024K
--------------------------------------------
Total memory      16,384K  14,764K    1,620K

Total under 1 MB     795K     199K      596K

Largest executable program size     596K (610,000 bytes)
Largest free upper memory block        0K     (0 bytes)
MS-DOS is resident in the high memory area.
```

You can also use Mem to see the names of the currently loaded device drivers and programs; add the /C switch. This usually generates a report that won't fit on a single screen, but if you add the /P switch, Mem pauses after each screenful until you press a key. Type *mem /c /p* to see a report like this:

```
Modules using memory below 1 MB:

Name         Total    =    Conventional  +   Upper Memory
---------------------------------------------------------
MSDOS      19,821  (19K)    19,821  (19K)        0    (0K)
HIMEM       1,168   (1K)     1,168   (1K)        0    (0K)
EMM386      3,120   (3K)     3,120   (3K)        0    (0K)
SETVER        592   (1K)       592   (1K)        0    (0K)
PROTMAN       128   (0K)       128   (0K)        0    (0K)
NE1000      9,072   (9K)     9,072   (9K)        0    (0K)
COMMAND     2,928   (3K)     2,928   (3K)        0    (0K)
NETWKSTA   47,936  (47K)    45,088  (44K)    2,848    (3K)
SMARTDRV   27,488  (27K)    27,488  (27K)        0    (0K)
MOUSE      14,928  (15K)    14,928  (15K)        0    (0K)
DOSKEY      4,144   (4K)     4,144   (4K)        0    (0K)
SNAPDIB     4,768   (5K)     4,768   (5K)        0    (0K)
DBLSPACE   39,472  (39K)         0   (0K)   39,472   (39K)
NETBEUI    36,208  (35K)         0   (0K)   36,208   (35K)
WORKGRP     4,400   (4K)         0   (0K)    4,400    (4K)
Free      548,512 (536K)   522,048 (510K)   26,464   (26K)

Memory Summary:

Press any key to continue . . .
```

MemMaker The MemMaker program optimizes (that is, it makes most effective use of) your computer's **memory**. It does this by examining upper memory and all of the installable **device drivers** and **memory-resident programs** that you load with **CONFIG.SYS** and **AUTOEXEC.BAT**, and then calculating the best way to load each driver and program so that the maximum amount of upper memory is used. This process, therefore, leaves the maximum amount of conventional memory available for use by other programs.

After MemMaker completes its analysis, it adds appropriate **DeviceHigh** and LH (**LoadHigh**) commands to your startup files. (In some cases, it also modifies the SYSTEM.INI file from your Windows directory.)

It's a complex process that, mercifully, requires only a simple explanation to use. Follow these steps to optimize memory with MemMaker:

1 At the command prompt, type *memmaker*. Press Enter after you read MemMaker's welcome screen.

2 MemMaker offers a choice between Express Setup and Custom Setup. Choose Express Setup and press Enter.

3 MemMaker asks if you have any programs that need expanded memory (EMS). If you're not sure, answer No.

4 MemMaker restarts your system two times and performs its magic. When it finishes, MemMaker reports on its success, like this:

```
Microsoft MemMaker

MemMaker has finished optimizing your system's memory. The following
table summarizes the memory use (in bytes) on your system:

                              Before      After
    Memory Type             MemMaker    MemMaker      Change

  Free conventional memory:   557,504     626,704      69,200

  Upper memory:
      Used by programs         29,024      98,224      69,200
      Reserved for Windows          0           0           0
      Reserved for EMS              0           0           0
      Free                    129,536      60,288

  Expanded memory:           Disabled    Disabled

Your original CONFIG.SYS and AUTOEXEC.BAT files have been saved
as CONFIG.UMB and AUTOEXEC.UMB.  If MemMaker changed your Windows
SYSTEM.INI file, the original file was saved as SYSTEM.UMB.

ENTER=Exit  ESC=Undo changes
```

If you later change your mind and want to restore your original setup files, type *memmaker /undo* at the command prompt.

continues

MemMaker *(continued)*

Do you use a menu program?

If your AUTOEXEC.BAT program starts a "shell" program that lets you launch programs, be sure you exit the shell after each time MemMaker restarts. If you don't see Memmaker's final report (shown above), it hasn't finished its job. Quit your shell.

What About Custom Setup?

If you choose Custom Setup instead of Express Setup, MemMaker displays an additional screen with several options, as shown below. Press F1 to see an explanation of each option, as well as advice on selecting the correct option for your situation.

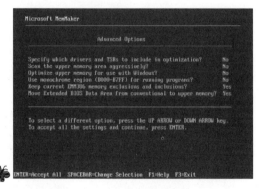

```
Microsoft MemMaker


                          Advanced Options


   Specify which drivers and TSRs to include in optimization?        No
   Scan the upper memory area aggressively?                          No
   Optimize upper memory for use with Windows?                       No
   Use monochrome region (B000-B7FF) for running programs?           No
   Keep current EMM386 memory exclusions and inclusions?             Yes
   Move Extended BIOS Data Area from conventional to upper memory?   Yes



   To select a different option, press the UP ARROW or DOWN ARROW key.
   To accept all the settings and continue, press ENTER.
                                         0


ENTER=Accept All  SPACEBAR=Change Selection  F1=Help  F3=Exit
```

Set it and forget it? Forget it!

If you make changes to your **CONFIG.SYS** or **AUTOEXEC.BAT** file (or you install a new program that changes either file), run MemMaker again.

Memory   Memory—sometimes called RAM, for "Random Access Memory"—is your computer's "workspace." When you use programs and data, MS-DOS copies the information from a disk to memory. It's important to understand the difference between disk storage and memory: Disk storage is (relatively) permanent, whereas the contents of memory are lost when you turn off your computer or **boot** it. Your computer can work with programs and files only when they are in memory; it can't work directly with disk files. (Some programs work with large files by copying only part of the file to memory at any one time and swapping other parts to disk.)

There's one other important thing to know about memory: You need lots of it! If you don't have enough, some programs won't run at all, and others will run slowly. But just having the memory in your system isn't enough; you must configure it properly and use it efficiently. To configure memory properly, use memory-managing device drivers such as **HIMEM.SYS** and **EMM386.EXE**. To use memory efficiently, eliminate any **device drivers** and **memory-resident programs** that you don't need, and load as many of the remaining drivers and programs in "upper" memory as possible. This maximizes the amount of free (available) "conventional" memory, which is the type that most programs use as their workspace.

To find out how much and what type of memory you need to run a particular program, check the program's documentation.

continues

Memory *(continued)*

Types of Memory

Perhaps the most confusing aspect of memory is the alphabet soup of memory types: XMS, EMS, HMA, UMB, VCPI, and so on. Here's all you really need to know:

Conventional memory	Every computer has conventional memory, which is the first 640 **KB** of memory. All MS-DOS–based programs require conventional memory.
Upper memory area	If your computer has more than 640 KB of memory, the area of memory from 640 KB up to 1 **MB** is called the upper memory area. It's used by system hardware, such as a display adapter. On computers with a 386, 486, or Pentium processor, you can also install device drivers and memory-resident programs into this area instead of conventional memory, where they would otherwise reside. Usable sections of the upper memory area are called "upper memory blocks" or UMBs.
Extended memory (also called XMS)	On computers with a 286, 386, 486, or Pentium processor, the memory above 1 MB is called extended memory. Windows and many programs require extended memory. Using extended memory requires an extended memory manager, such as HIMEM.SYS.
High memory area (HMA)	The first 64 KB of extended memory is called the high memory area. You can use the DOS command to load MS-DOS into this area to conserve conventional memory.

Expanded memory (EMS *or* EMS/VCPI)	Expanded memory is installed on an expanded-memory board, and is usually found only on computers with an 8088 processor. (Newer computers use extended memory, which is faster.) Many programs require expanded memory, but you can run them on a computer that has only extended memory: You must use EMM386.EXE, which uses extended memory to simulate expanded memory.

Checking memory usage—**Mem**

Using high memory—**DeviceHigh; LoadHigh; DOS; EMM386.EXE; HIMEM.SYS**

Optimizing memory usage—**MemMaker**

Memory-Resident Program
A memory-resident program is one that loads into memory and remains there—usually until you restart your computer. (Ordinary programs, such as word processors and spreadsheets, remove themselves from memory when you exit the program.) Memory-resident programs usually wait in the wings until some event, such as pressing a special key combination or deleting a file, prompts them to act. Memory-resident programs are sometimes called TSRs, for "Terminate and Stay Resident."

 Mem

MenuColor   The MenuColor command specifies the colors to use for the startup menu if you use **multiple configurations**. If you want to use colors other than white on black, place this command under the [**Menu**] header in **CONFIG.SYS.** Available colors are numbered 0 through 15, as shown in the table below. You can specify a foreground color and a background color; separate the two numbers with a comma, like this:

```
menucolor=15,1
```

Number	Color	Number	Color
0	Black	8	Gray
1	Blue	9	Bright blue
2	Green	10	Bright green
3	Cyan	11	Bright cyan
4	Red	12	Bright red
5	Magenta	13	Bright magenta
6	Brown	14	Yellow
7	White	15	Bright white

MenuDefault   The MenuDefault command specifies the default choice in the startup menu if you use **multiple configurations**. The default choice is automatically highlighted, so that you can select it simply by pressing Enter. You can also use this command to tell MS-DOS to use the default choice if the user doesn't make a selection within a time you define. Place this command under the [**Menu**] header in **CONFIG.SYS.** For example, to tell MS-DOS to automatically select the DOS_Only configuration block after waiting 30 seconds for the user to make a choice, use this command:

```
menudefault=dos_only,30
```

[Menu] Header   The [Menu] header is used in **CONFIG.SYS** to define the startup menu if you want to use **multiple configurations.** Under the [Menu] header, you can use **MenuItem**, **MenuColor**, and **MenuDefault** commands.

MenuItem   The MenuItem command defines a menu item in the startup menu if you use **multiple configurations.** For each menu item, you specify the name of the configuration block to use if the user selects the menu item and, optionally, the text you want to appear in the startup menu. (If you don't specify text for the menu, MS-DOS displays the name of the configuration block in the menu.) Place the MenuItem commands under the [Menu] header in CONFIG.SYS.

Microsoft Anti-Virus   🐾 **Anti-Virus**

Microsoft Backup   🐾 **Backup**

Microsoft Tools Program Group

When you install MS-DOS version 6 on a computer that already has Microsoft Windows installed, the Setup program adds a new program group to Program Manager in Windows. The group includes icons for starting three programs:

Undelete for Windows

Anti-Virus for Windows

Backup for Windows

Installing Windows after you install MS-DOS

If you install Microsoft Windows after you install MS-DOS (or you chose not to install the Windows-based utilities when you installed MS-DOS), your Program Manager won't have this program group and icons. To add them, exit Windows, insert disk 1 of your original MS-DOS version 6 disks into your floppy drive, and type *a:setup /e*. The MS-DOS Setup program installs the Windows-based versions of Anti-Virus, Backup, and Undelete, adds a Microsoft Tools program group, and adds a **File Manager Tools menu**.

Microsoft Undelete ⁂ Undelete

Mirror

The Mirror command assists in recovering deleted or damaged files. Mirror is available only with MS-DOS version 5; in version 6 the **Delete Sentry** and **Delete Tracker** features of **Undelete** serve the same purpose. If you upgraded from version 5 to version 6, however, your **AUTOEXEC.BAT** file might still contain a reference to Mirror. You should delete the reference (replace it with an Undelete command if you want better Undelete protection) and delete the Mirror files: MIRROR.COM (in the DOS directory), MIRROR.FIL, and MIRROR.BAK (in the root directory).

MkDir ❖ MD

Mode

The Mode command provides several hardware-related functions. You can use it to configure and select serial ports, parallel (printer) ports, the display, and the keyboard.

Displaying More Lines on Your Screen

Normally, your monitor displays 25 lines of text. If you have an EGA or VGA display, you can squeeze more lines of text on the screen with this variant of the Mode command. For it to work, you must install **ANSI.SYS**. Valid values for the number of lines are 25, 43, and 50. For example:

```
mode con lines=43
```

Configuring a Serial Port

Most communications programs can properly set up a serial port for use with a modem. But if you have a printer or other device attached to a serial port, you might need to specify its communications parameters. For each serial port, you can set the baud rate, parity, number of data bits, number of stop bits, and retry action. For example:

```
mode com1 baud=2400 parity=n data=8 stop=1
```

Using a Serial-Interface Printer

Some applications allow you to print only to a printer attached to a parallel port, such as LPT1. If you have such an application and a serial-interface printer, you need Mode. Mode intercepts information directed to the parallel port and redirects it to your serial port. Before you use the following Mode command, you need to use another Mode command to configure the serial port (as described above) to match your printer's communication settings.

```
mode lpt1=com1
```

continues

Mode *(continued)*

Configuring a Printer

If you have an IBM-compatible or Epson-compatible printer, you can use the Mode command to set it to 80 or 132 columns per line, and 6 or 8 lines per inch. Most word processors and other applications make their own settings, but these settings are useful when you print directly from MS-DOS (printing a **Dir** listing, for example). A Mode command that squeezes a lot of text on the page looks like this:

```
mode lpt1 cols=132 lines=8
```

More

The More command pauses a scrolling display after every screenful and waits for you to press a key. You can use it to display a file or control the output from an MS-DOS command.

Displaying a File One Screenful at a Time

To display a file with More, you use a **redirection** symbol to specify the file as input to the More command. For example, to display a file named README.TXT, type this:

```
more < readme.txt
```

Controlling Command Output

Some MS-DOS commands, such as **Dir** and **Mem**, have a /P switch that causes the display to pause after each screenful, awaiting your keystroke. Other commands can also generate a lot of text on the screen, but they don't provide a way to stop it. With **piping**, you can use More to do just that. For example:

```
sort parts.lst | more
```

Move The Move command moves one or more files from one directory to another—on the same disk or on another disk. To do so, you specify the file and the name of the directory that you want to move the file to, like this:

```
move seinfeld.doc \tv\sitcom
```

This command moves the SEINFELD.DOC file to the SITCOM directory. If a file by that name already exists in the SITCOM directory, Move asks if you want to overwrite (replace) the existing file.

To move more than one file, separate the **filenames** with a comma or use **wildcard** characters in the **file specification**. For example:

```
move sam.doc,dave.doc \fanmail
```

Move can also rename

If you include a filename as part of the destination, the Move command moves the file and renames it—but you can use this trick only if you're moving a single file.

The renaming ability also has another use: renaming directories. (The **Ren** command can rename files, but not directories.) If you specify a directory name as the source instead of a filename, Move renames the directory. Although you can change the name of a directory, you can't change its location in the directory tree; to do that, use **XCopy**.

Mscdex   The Mscdex command provides access to a **CD-ROM drive.** (By the way, "Mscdex" is not a secret code or aboriginal language; it's abbreviated from "*Microsoft CD-ROM Ex*tensions.") If you use a CD-ROM drive, your **CONFIG.SYS** file must contain a **Device** or **DeviceHigh** command that loads the **device driver** that came with your CD-ROM drive. It might look like this, for example:

```
devicehigh=c:\cdrom\fdcd.sys /d:mscd001 /t
```

The /D parameter provides the "driver signature," and it must be repeated in the Mscdex command, which you put in your **AUTOEXEC.BAT** file, like this:

```
c:\dos\mscdex /d:mscd001 /l:g
```

The /L switch, which is optional, lets you specify the drive letter for the first CD-ROM drive. In this example, only one CD-ROM drive is installed, and its drive letter is G.

Use SMARTDrive to speed up CD-ROM access

SMARTDrive, the disk caching program that comes with MS-DOS, can speed up access to your CD-ROM drive by storing previously read information. To use this feature, the Mscdex command must appear *before* the Smartdrv command in your AUTOEXEC.BAT file.

MSD The MSD (for "Microsoft Diagnostics") program displays information about your computer, such as the type of processor and display adapter it has, amount and type of memory, number of serial ports, and so on. To see this display, type *msd* at the command prompt.

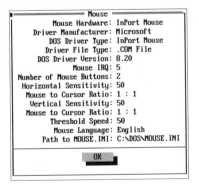

```
 File  Utilities  Help

   Computer...    American Megatrend      Disk Drives...    A: B: C: D:
                  486DX                                     P:

   Memory...      640K, 15360K Ext,       LPT Ports...      1
                  12924K XMS

   Video...       UGA, Radius             COM Ports...      2
                  SVGA

   Network...     No Network              IRQ Status...

   OS Version...  MS-DOS Version 6.20     TSR Programs...

   Mouse...       InPort Mouse 8.20       Device Drivers...

   Other Adapters...  Game Adapter

 Press ALT for menu, or press highlighted letter, or F3 to quit MSD.
```

For more detailed information about any displayed item, click the button next to that item or press its highlighted letter. A window of detailed, cryptic, technical information appears, like this:

```
                    ═══ Mouse ═══
            Mouse Hardware: InPort Mouse
       Driver Manufacturer: Microsoft
           DOS Driver Type: InPort Mouse
          Driver File Type: .COM File
        DOS Driver Version: 8.20
                 Mouse IRQ: 5
   Number of Mouse Buttons: 2
     Horizontal Sensitivity: 50
       Mouse to Cursor Ratio: 1 : 1
        Vertical Sensitivity: 50
       Mouse to Cursor Ratio: 1 : 1
           Threshold Speed: 50
            Mouse Language: English
         Path to MOUSE.INI: C:\DOS\MOUSE.INI

                     ▌ OK ▐
```

MS-DOS–Based Application
An MS-DOS–based application is one that requires MS-DOS—but not Windows—to run.

:· **Windows-Based Application**

MS-DOS Editor :· **Editor**

MS-DOS Help :· **Help**

MS-DOS Shell
MS-DOS Shell is a full-screen graphical interface for MS-DOS—an alternative to the command prompt. With MS-DOS Shell, you can perform many of the same operations that MS-DOS commands perform—such as viewing, copying, moving, and deleting files and directories—without learning MS-DOS commands. Instead, you point and click with the mouse or choose commands from drop-down menus.

MS-DOS Shell is included with MS-DOS versions 4.0 through 6.0. If you have version 6.2 or later, you can get MS-DOS Shell by ordering the **Supplemental Disk.** To use MS-DOS Shell, type *dosshell* at the command prompt. You'll see a display something like this:

Menu bar — Drive pane — Directory Tree pane — File List pane — Program List pane

To use the menu bar, press and hold down the Alt key and then press the first letter of the menu name to open a menu. Release both keys, and then press the underlined letter of the command name to choose a command.

The drive pane displays the name of the **current directory** and an icon for each available **disk drive**. Use the direction keys to highlight a drive letter, and then press Spacebar to make it the **current drive**.

The directory tree pane displays the names of the directories on the current drive. Use the Up and Down direction keys to move the highlight and change the current directory. Use the Plus and Minus keys to expand or collapse the list of subdirectories.

The file list pane displays the names of the files in the current directory. Commands that you choose from the menu affect the highlighted file(s) in this pane.

The program list pane displays the names of program items, which start a program, and the names of other program lists. You can create your own program items, enabling you to choose programs from a menu instead of typing a command at the command prompt.

Press Tab to move the highlight from one pane to another, or simply click the mouse in the pane you want to use. You can get more detailed help about using MS-DOS Shell by choosing a topic from the Help menu.

To quit MS-DOS Shell and return to the good ol' command prompt, choose Exit from the File menu.

Running several programs with MS-DOS Shell

In addition to the file-management and program-launching abilities of MS-DOS Shell, it also enables **Task Swapper**, which lets you switch among several programs without quitting one and starting another. To use this feature, choose Enable Task Swapper from the Options menu. Then when you start a program, MS-DOS Shell adds it to the Active Task list. You can switch from one program to the next by pressing Alt+Tab.

Multiple Configurations

Multiple configurations is a feature of MS-DOS versions 6 and later that allows you to set up more than one set of commands in your CONFIG.SYS file, and then choose which set you want to use whenever you **boot** your computer.

Because the device drivers and other CONFIG.SYS settings affect the amount of free memory for programs, you might want to have separate configurations for different tasks you want to perform. Network drivers, for example, require a lot of memory, and may not leave enough memory free for playing your favorite video game; you could set up separate configurations for connecting to the network and for playing games.

Setting Up Multiple Configurations

1 Use **Editor** to open CONFIG.SYS.

2 Define the startup menu, which appears each time you boot your computer. The definition must begin with a **[Menu] header**, and contains one **MenuItem** command for each configuration. Optionally, you can include **Submenu, MenuColor**, and **MenuDefault** commands. This block, like the sample below, should appear at the beginning of your CONFIG.SYS file.

```
[menu]
menuitem=Net, Use network
menuitem=Games, Play games
menucolor=15,1
menudefault=Net, 15
```

3 Define a configuration block for each configuration. The block begins with a block header—the block name enclosed between square brackets. The configuration block includes all the commands that you want to use for that configuration. For example:

```
[net]
files=60
device=c:\net\network.sys
lastdrive=s

[games]
files=30
device=c:\sound\sound.sys
```

4 You can also define a [common] configuration block; its commands always execute, regardless of the startup menu selection.

```
[common]
device=c:\dos\himem.sys
device=c:\dos\emm386.exe noems
dos=high, umb
```

5 Save CONFIG.SYS. If you don't need **AUTOEXEC.BAT** to execute certain commands depending on which configuration is selected, go to Step 9.

6 If you want different parts of your AUTOEXEC.BAT program to execute depending on which configuration is selected, open AUTOEXEC.BAT in Editor. Add a line that tells MS-DOS to branch to the appropriate section of AUTOEXEC.BAT:

```
goto %config%
```

7 Add a label and the commands you want to execute for each configuration.

```
:net
netmenu
goto end

:games
cd \games
explodem

:end
```

8 Save AUTOEXEC.BAT.

9 Exit Editor and restart your computer.

Using Multiple Configurations

After you set up multiple configurations as described above, you'll see a startup menu like this whenever you boot your computer:

```
MS-DOS 6.2 Startup Menu


   1. Use network
   2. Play games

Enter a choice: 1      Time remaining: 15
```

Use the direction keys or press the number of the menu item you want, and then press Enter. In our example, if you don't make a selection within 15 seconds, the Net configuration block is selected by default.

⁘ Include

Multitasking ❖ MS-DOS Shell; Task Swapper

NumLock

The NumLock command turns your keyboard's Num Lock feature on or off when you **boot** your computer. When Num Lock is on (usually indicated by a light on the keyboard), the keypad at the right side of the keyboard can be used for typing numbers. When Num Lock is off, the keys can be used for moving the cursor. (In either case, you can get the other function by holding Shift while you press a key.)

The NumLock command can be used only in **CONFIG.SYS**. To turn NumLock on, use the command *numlock=on* in CONFIG.SYS; to turn NumLock off, use *numlock=off*.

Save a keystroke!

If you use **multiple configurations**, place a *numlock=on* command under the **[Menu] header**. This ensures that Num Lock is on when the startup menu of numbered choices appears.

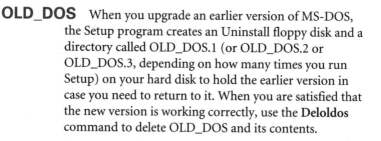

OLD_DOS

When you upgrade an earlier version of MS-DOS, the Setup program creates an Uninstall floppy disk and a directory called OLD_DOS.1 (or OLD_DOS.2 or OLD_DOS.3, depending on how many times you run Setup) on your hard disk to hold the earlier version in case you need to return to it. When you are satisfied that the new version is working correctly, use the **Deloldos** command to delete OLD_DOS and its contents.

❖ **Uninstall**

Parameters A parameter is some information that you include on a command line in addition to the command name. It can be a qualifier—such as a drive, directory, or filename—that makes a command more specific, or a "switch" that enables a certain feature of the command. For example:

```
dir c:\*.bak /p
    Parameters
```

Commands used in **batch programs** and **Doskey** macros can also use "replaceable parameters." A replaceable parameter acts as a placeholder for the actual parameter, which you supply when you run the batch program or macro.

Using Replaceable Parameters in Batch Programs

To use a replaceable parameter as part of a command in a batch program, type a percent sign (%) followed by a number from 1 through 9. When you run the batch program, the first parameter you type on the command line replaces %1, the second parameter replaces %2, and so on.

Here's a short batch file, called UPDATE.BAT, that shows how replaceable parameters work:

```
copy %1.wks lastmo.wks
copy %2.wks thismo.wks
```

If you type *update jan feb* at the command prompt, the first line in the batch program copies the file JAN.WKS to the file LASTMO.WKS. The next line copies FEB.WKS to THISMO.WKS.

continues

Parameters *(continued)*

Using filenames and commands with percent signs

To refer to files that contain % as part of their name (such as %PROFIT.XLS) in a batch program, you must type the filename with two percent signs: %%PROFIT.XLS. To use a replaceable parameter in a batch-program **For** command, such as *for %a in (*.bat) do print %a*, you must type two percent signs: *for %%a in (*.bat) do print %%a*.

Using Replaceable Parameters in Doskey Macros

To use a replaceable parameter as part of a Doskey macro, type a dollar sign ($) followed by a number from 1 through 9. When you run the macro, the first parameter you type on the command line replaces $1, the second parameter replaces $2, and so on.

Parent Directory
A parent directory is the directory within which a **subdirectory** is contained. For example, if the **pathname** of the LETTERS directory is C:\PERSONAL\LETTERS, then PERSONAL is the parent directory of LETTERS and C:\ (the **root directory** on drive C) is the parent of PERSONAL. You can use two periods (..) as an abbreviation for the parent directory of the **current directory**.

 . and ..; Path

Path

The Path command displays or sets the list of directories that MS-DOS searches to find a program file when the file is not in the **current directory**. This list of directories is called the *search path*. To display the current search path, type *path* at the command prompt. To set the search path, type *path* followed by a list of directories (each with its complete **pathname**) separated by semicolons. For example:

```
path c:\dos;c:\dos\bat;c:\word
```

After you execute this command, if you type the name of a program that isn't in the current directory, MS-DOS looks for the program file in the DOS directory, then in the BAT directory, and then in the WORD directory.

Getting lost on the path?

The maximum length of the Path command is 127 characters. If you need to include many pathnames (or a few long pathnames), you can quickly exceed this limit. To solve the problem, use the **Subst** command to change the names of some of your paths to drive letters. For example, after you type *subst w: c:\programs\wordproc\word*, you can shorten your Path command from

```
path c:\dos;c:\programs\wordproc\word
```
to
```
path c:\dos;w:\
```

The Path command is usually executed from a batch program, particularly **AUTOEXEC.BAT**. But you can use it at the command prompt as well.

Pathname

A pathname is the complete list of directories that locates a **subdirectory** on a disk. A pathname always starts with the **root directory** and separates each subdirectory with a backslash. For example, *c:\safari\kenya\graphics*.

∴ **File Specification**

Pause   The Pause command is used in **batch programs**. It displays the message "Press any key to continue . . ." and waits for the user to press a key before executing the next command in the batch program. When a key other than **Ctrl+C** or **Ctrl+Break** is pressed, execution of the batch file continues. (Pressing Ctrl+C or Ctrl+Break allows you to stop execution of the batch program. The message "Terminate batch job (Y/N)?" appears; press Y to quit the batch program, or press N to continue execution.)

To display a more descriptive message, use an **Echo** command just before Pause in your batch program.

Piping   Piping is a way of using the output of one command as the input for another. You use the vertical bar or "pipe" (¦) between two commands to send the output from the first command to the second. Typical uses are to "pipe" the output from the **Dir**, **Type**, or **Find** command to the **More** command. For example,

```
find "MS-DOS" c:\dos\readme.txt ¦ more
```

searches through the file README.TXT for lines containing "MS-DOS" and sends the output to the More command, which displays it one screen at a time.

 Redirection

Power Management   MS-DOS version 6 provides a power management scheme that conserves energy when applications and hardware devices are idle. This is especially useful if you are using a laptop or notebook computer that runs on batteries.

To use power management, you must load the POWER.EXE **device driver** with a **Device** command in **CONFIG.SYS**. After POWER.EXE is loaded, you can use the Power command to control the degree of power conservation you want.

Loading the POWER.EXE Device Driver

POWER.EXE provides several power conservation options, which vary the degree of conservation:

- *adv:max* provides maximum power conservation

- *adv:reg* provides a balance between power conservation and system performance

- *adv:min* provides minimum power conservation for applications that do not perform satisfactorily at the higher settings

- *std* uses the power-management features built in to your computer (If your computer does not provide built-in power management, *std* turns off power management.)

- *off* turns off power management

To load POWER.EXE, put the following line in your CONFIG.SYS file. At the end of the line, type a space and the power conservation option you want:

```
device=c:\dos\power.exe adv:reg
```

Using the Power Command

After the POWER.EXE device driver is loaded, you can check on or change the power-conservation option with the Power command. Type *power* at the command prompt to display the current power conservation option. You'll see a display like this:

```
C:\>power

Power Management Status
-----------------------
Setting = ADV: REG
CPU: idle 57% of time.
```

Type *power* followed by a space and any one of the power conservation options above to set that power option.

Print   The Print command, as you might expect, prints a file.
              However, it prints only plain unformatted text files, such
              as those you create with **Editor.** If you try to use Print
              with a word processor file or other formatted file, your
              printer prints gibberish or nothing at all. (Print is also
              persnickety about the type of printer you have. It won't
              work with a PostScript printer.)

              Print is actually a small program that loads into memory
              the first time that you use it, and stays there until you
              reboot your computer. It acts as a *print buffer* or *spooler*
              that allows printing to take place in the background while
              you work on other tasks. It also allows you to queue up
              multiple files for printing one after the other.

              Setting the Printer Port

              The first time in a session that you use Print, you must tell it which
              port your printer is attached to. At the command prompt, type *print.*
              This message appears:

              ```
              Name of list device [PRN]:
              ```

              Press Enter to use the first parallel port (LPT1). Or type the name of the
              port your printer is attached to: LPT2 or LPT3 for a parallel printer or
              COM1 through COM4 for a serial printer. When Print is ready to work,
              it responds:

              ```
              Resident part of PRINT installed

              PRINT queue is empty
              ```

              Printing

              After you set the printer port, Print is very simple to use: type *print*
              followed by a space and the name of a file, and press Enter. You can
              also specify a list of files to print, each separated by a space, or you
              can use **wildcard** characters to specify multiple files.

Canceling Printing

When you tell Print to print a file, it places the file in its *print queue*, a list of files waiting to be printed, until the printer is ready to receive the data. If you change your mind about printing, you can remove one or all of the files from this print queue.

To remove a particular file from the print queue, type *print* followed by a space, the **file specification**, and */c*. For example:

```
print jungle.txt /c
```

To remove all of the files from the print queue, type *print /t*.

More ways to print

MS-DOS provides two other ways to send information to your printer: the **Copy** command and **redirection**.

To print with the Copy command, simply use the port your printer is attached to as the destination for the file(s), like this:

```
copy tarzan.txt lpt1
```

To use redirection to print, use the > redirection symbol followed by the port your printer is attached to. Use this trick to get a printed copy of a **Dir** listing, for example:

```
dir > lpt1
```

Printing the contents of the display

Another way to print a **Dir** listing or any other information that appears on your screen is to send a "snapshot" of the screen image to the printer. Press PrtSc to do so. (If you want to print a graphical image displayed on your screen, you must first load the **Graphics** program.) Note that if you print to a page printer (such as a laser printer), the screen text won't print until you print enough screens to fill a page or send a command to print the page; you can use the **Echo** command to do that.

Memory-Resident Program

Prompt The Prompt command sets the command prompt. It is usually used in **batch programs**, particularly **AUTOEXEC.BAT,** but you can use it at the command prompt. Any changes Prompt makes to the command prompt take effect as soon as you press Enter.

When you install or upgrade MS-DOS, it inserts the Prompt command *prompt pg* in your AUTOEXEC.BAT file. This sets the command prompt to the **current drive** and **current directory**, followed by a greater than sign, like this:

```
C:\>
```

To have your prompt display other information, such as the date and time, use the Prompt command followed by one or more of the dollar-sign codes in the following table. For example, this command changes the prompt to the date and time on two lines, followed by the current drive and directory on a third line:

```
prompt $d$_$t$_$p$g
```
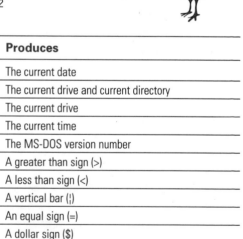
```
Mon 01-17-1994
12:31:15.12
C:\DOS>
```

Code	Produces
$D	The current date
$P	The current drive and current directory
$N	The current drive
$T	The current time
$V	The MS-DOS version number
$G	A greater than sign (>)
$L	A less than sign (<)
$B	A vertical bar (¦)
$Q	An equal sign (=)
$$	A dollar sign ($)
$H	A backspace
$_	A signal to end the current line and begin a new one
$E	An escape code (ASCII 27); use this to enter **ANSI.SYS** control sequences

To use other text in your command prompt, include it after the Prompt command without a dollar sign. For example:

```
prompt This is my computer $g
This is my computer >
```

If you type *prompt* by itself with no codes or text, MS-DOS changes the prompt to the current drive (without the current directory) followed by a greater than sign, like this: C>.

No prompt at all

Prompt followed by a dollar sign and any character except those in the table (or a dollar sign alone) displays the cursor by itself. You can use this trick to make the prompt disappear altogether. For example, type

```
prompt $a
```

and you have nothing but a blinking cursor for a prompt. (Use *prompt pg* to return to the standard prompt.)

QBasic   The QBasic command starts the QBasic interpreter, which allows you to create programs in the QBasic programming language. Using the QBasic programming language is a topic for an entire book itself and is beyond the scope of this Field Guide.

Running MS-DOS QBasic by Michael Halvorson and David Rygmyr (Microsoft Press, 1991) is a good source of information on QBasic.

If you're not a programmer

Even if you never plan to use QBasic, do not delete the QBASIC.EXE file from your DOS directory. The MS-DOS **Editor**, which you will probably use, needs QBASIC.EXE to run.

RAMDrive

RAMDrive is a **device driver** that creates a "RAM drive." A RAM drive is a section of **memory** (RAM) you designate to simulate a **disk drive**. Because memory is much faster than a hard drive, using a RAM drive can be an advantage when you want to quickly store and retrieve information, such as when you are updating a database or storing temporary files.

Using a RAM drive also has disadvantages, however. Information in a RAM drive is lost when you shut down or restart your computer. You must remember to save the contents of a RAM drive to a real disk before you shut down or restart. Another consideration is that a RAM drive sets aside a sizable portion of your computer's memory, which may be needed for other purposes.

Creating a RAM Drive

To create a RAM drive, add a **Device** or **DeviceHigh** command to your **CONFIG.SYS** file, like this:

```
device=c:\dos\ramdrive.sys
```

This creates a 64-**KB** RAM drive and assigns it the next available drive letter. You can specify the size of the RAM drive, from 4 KB to 32767 KB (32 **MB**) if you have the memory available, by adding the size (in KB) you want to the command line, like this:

```
device=c:\dos\ramdrive.sys 256
```

By default, MS-DOS creates RAM drives in conventional memory. Because this is the memory required to run programs, it is generally better to create a RAM drive in extended or expanded memory. To create a RAM drive in extended memory, add /E at the end of the Device command line. To create a RAM drive in expanded memory, add /A.

Install your memory manager first

If you use the /E or /A options when creating a RAM drive, be sure to place *device=ramdrive.sys* in your CONFIG.SYS file after the lines that enable extended or expanded memory.

RD

The RD command—short for "Remove Directory"—deletes a directory. To remove a directory, type *rd* and the full **pathname** of the directory. For example:

```
rd \word\letters
```

A directory must be completely empty before MS-DOS allows you to delete it. If the directory you specify contains any files or subdirectories, you will see the message "Invalid path, not directory, or directory not empty." Delete or move any files or subdirectories contained in the directory and retry. Another possibility is that the directory you specified is the **current directory**. Type *cd ..* to change to the **parent directory** and retry.

But it *looks* empty!

If the directory you want to remove appears to be empty, but MS-DOS still displays the "not empty" message, use the **Attrib** command to check for hidden or system files.

CD; Del; DelTree; Move

Read-Only Attribute   **Attrib; File Attributes**

Redirection   Redirection changes where an MS-DOS command gets its input or sends its output.

Redirecting Input

Most MS-DOS commands get their input from you, via the keyboard. Use the < symbol to tell a command to get its input somewhere else, such as from a file. For example,

```
sort < sales.txt
```

tells the **Sort** command to get its input (the data to be sorted) from the SALES.TXT file instead of from the keyboard.

Redirecting Output

Most MS-DOS commands send their output to the screen. Use the > symbol to tell a command to send its output somewhere else, such as to the printer or to a disk file. For example,

```
dir > prn
```

tells the **Dir** command to send its output (the directory listing) to the printer instead of to the screen.

Redirecting Input and Output

In some cases, you might want to redirect both the input to and output from a command. You can do both on the same command line. After the command, add the < symbol followed by the source for the input, followed by the > symbol, followed by the destination for the output. For example,

```
sort < sales.txt > prn
```

sorts the file SALES.TXT and sends the sorted output directly to the printer.

 Piping

Rem

The Rem command (short for "remark") is used in **batch programs** and the **CONFIG.SYS** file to insert comments, reminders, or explanations. Type *rem* at the beginning of a line followed by any text you want. When you execute the file, MS-DOS ignores the line. The comment line can be up to 127 characters long (including the word *rem* and any spaces).

Rem is also a handy way to "comment out" commands from your batch programs while you are testing or modifying them. If you insert Rem at the beginning of the line, MS-DOS ignores any commands on the rest of the line. If you want to reactivate the command line at a later time, simply delete the word *rem*.

One more comment

In MS-DOS version 6, you can use a semicolon (;) instead of Rem at the beginning of a line in CONFIG.SYS to comment out a command. This works only for CONFIG.SYS, however; you must still use Rem for your batch programs.

Ren

The Ren command (short for "Rename"), as you might expect, changes a file's name. To use it, type *ren* followed by the current **filename**, followed by the new name. For example, *ren leopard.bmp lion.bmp* changes the name of that picture of a big cat. (Who says a leopard can't change its spots?)

You can use **wildcard** characters with Ren to change the names of several files. For example, *ren *.txt *.doc* changes the names of all the files with a TXT extension to the same names with a DOC extension.

Renaming directories

Ren works only for files, not for directory names. To rename a directory, use the **Move** command. For example, *move c:\journey c:\trip* renames the directory C:\JOURNEY to C:\TRIP.

 Label

Rename ❖ Ren

Replace

The Replace command lets you replace files in one or more directories with identically named files from a source that you specify. For example, *replace a:*.** replaces all files in the **current directory** with the files of the same name on the disk in drive A. You can also specify a directory for the files that will be replaced. For example, *replace a:*.** c:\personal* replaces all files in the C:\PERSONAL directory with the like-named files on the disk in drive A.

Updating Files

You can use Replace with its /U (update) switch to replace files only when the source files have a more recent date and time. For example,

```
replace a:*.doc c:\letters /u
```

updates the files in the C:\LETTERS directory with the like-named DOC files on drive A that have a more recent date and time.

Adding Files

You can use Replace with its /A (add) switch to add specified files to a directory only when like-named files do not already exist in the target directory. For example,

```
replace a:*.doc c:\letters /a
```

adds to the C:\LETTERS directory all the DOC files on drive A that do not already exist in C:\LETTERS.

You want more?

Replace has several more switches that let you customize how it works:

/S	Applies the replacement to all subdirectories contained in the target directory
/R	Extends the replacement to include files with the read-only **file attribute**
/P	Prompts you for confirmation before it replaces or adds each file
/W	Prompts you to press a key before the replacement begins (so you can insert a floppy disk, for example)

⁘ **Copy; XCopy**

Resource Kit   The MS-DOS 6 Resource Kit provides additional
information about MS-DOS—more than you'll find in
the MS-DOS package, its online Help, and this Field
Guide combined. The Resource Kit includes the *MS-DOS
6 Technical Reference*, which provides a detailed printed
reference for all the MS-DOS commands and technical
information about **DoubleSpace** and **MemMaker**. In addition, the Resource Kit includes the **Supplemental Disk**,
which you can obtain separately if you don't need the
printed documentation.

The Resource Kit is a nice addendum for intrepid
explorers who got their feet wet with this Field Guide. To
order it, send in the coupon at the back of your MS-DOS
manual, or call Microsoft Sales at (800) 426-9400 (U.S.)
or (800) 563-9048 (Canada).

Restore   The Restore command restores files from backups created with the **Backup** command included with MS-DOS versions 5 and earlier. If you have version 6.0 or later, use Microsoft Backup (or its Windows version) to back up and restore files. The Restore command will not restore files backed up with Microsoft Backup.

To restore a file, insert the backup disk into a floppy drive and type *restore* followed by the letter of the drive containing the backup files and the **file specification** for the file(s) to be restored. Restore always restores files to the same directory from which they were originally backed up. For example, *restore a: c:\letters\ *.doc* restores all the DOC files from the backup disk in drive A to the C:\LETTERS directory.

You can use the following switches to modify the Restore command:

/S	Restores files to all subdirectories within the specified directory
/P	Prompts you to confirm restoration of a read-only file or a file that has changed since it was backed up
/M	Restores only files that have been modified since they were backed up
/N	Restores only files that do not exist in the destination directory—that is, files that have been deleted since they were backed up
/D	Displays a list of the files on the backup disk that match the filenames you specify without restoring them
/B:*date*	Restores only files on the backup disk with dates on or before the date you specify
/A:*date*	Restores only files on the backup disk with dates on or after the date you specify
/E:*time*	Restores only files on the backup disk with times equal to or earlier than the time you specify
/L:*time*	Restores only files on the backup disk with times equal to later than the time you specify

   Attrib; File Attributes

RmDir ❖ RD

Root Directory

Every **floppy disk** and hard disk has a root directory. It is the disk's main or top **directory**, which contains all other directories and **subdirectories**. MS-DOS identifies the root directory with a single backslash (\). Thus, C:\ is the root directory of the hard disk C. You cannot name or delete a disk's root directory. (But you can name the disk itself with the **Label** command.)

Although subdirectories contained within the root can hold an unlimited number of files and other subdirectories, the root directory itself is limited in the number of entries it can hold. On a double-density (360-KB or 720-KB) floppy disk, the root can hold a maximum of 112 file and directory entries; a high-density (1.2-**MB** or 1.44-MB) floppy, 224 entries. A root directory on a hard disk can hold a maximum of 512 entries, regardless of the capacity of the hard disk—which is one reason to use subdirectories.

❖ **Directory; Subdirectory**

ScanDisk

ScanDisk is a program that takes a close-up look at your disk and corrects any problems that it finds. ScanDisk is included with MS-DOS version 6.2.

Checking a Disk with ScanDisk

To use ScanDisk, type *scandisk* at the command prompt. You'll see a screen that displays the tasks that ScanDisk performs on your disk. As ScanDisk completes each task, a checkmark appears next to that task on the screen. (If yours is a **DoubleSpace** drive, you'll see a few extra items on ScanDisk's task list not shown in the illustation here.)

```
Microsoft ScanDisk

ScanDisk is now checking the following areas of drive D:

  √    Media descriptor
  »    File allocation tables
       Directory structure
       File system
       Surface scan




  ‹ Pause ›   ‹ More Info ›   ‹ Exit ›

  59% complete  ▓▓▓▓▓▓▓▓▓▓▓▓▓▓▓▓
```

ScanDisk and DoubleSpace

You can check DoubleSpace drives with ScanDisk. When you do, ScanDisk offers to first check the DoubleSpace drive's host drive. Checking the host drive is not absolutely necessary, but pressing Y to accept ScanDisk's offer gives you the most thorough checkup.

To Surface Scan or Not to Surface Scan

The last task that ScanDisk performs, called a surface scan, is a detailed examination of the entire surface of your disk. Depending on the size of your disk and the speed of your computer, a surface scan can take up to 30 minutes or more, so ScanDisk displays a box asking whether or not you want a surface scan.

A surface scan is often not necessary, but if you've received error messages when you tried to save or retrieve information recently, press Y to perform a surface scan. Otherwise, press N to skip the surface scan.

Fixing Disk Errors

When ScanDisk finds something wrong with your disk, it displays a box on the screen explaining what the problem is and offers you the option of fixing the problem. To repair the disk, select the Fix It option.

Search Path ⁂ Path

Serial Number

When you format a **floppy disk**, the **Format** command assigns a unique serial number to the disk. You can see the serial number by using the **Dir, ChkDsk, Label**, or **Vol** commands—but you can't change it or do anything useful with it.

Set

The Set command is used in batch programs and in **CONFIG.SYS** to define an **environment variable** that programs can use to tailor themselves to your system. Most programs automatically add the environment variable definitions they need to your **AUTOEXEC.BAT** or CONFIG.SYS file during their setup. For example, many programs use an environment variable called TEMP, which defines the directory used for storing temporary information. You will most likely find a line in your AUTOEXEC.BAT file something like *set temp=c:\temp*.

To define an environment variable, use the MS-DOS **Editor** to place a line in your AUTOEXEC.BAT or other **batch program**, like this: *set name=value*. Substitute whatever *name* you want to define and whatever *value* you want to assign.

You can also use Set to display the current environment variables and their values. At the command prompt, type *set* by itself and press Enter.

SetVer The SetVer **device driver**, SETVER.EXE, lets you use old
programs that were written specifically for an earlier
MS-DOS version. When you start one of these programs,
the program refuses to run unless its expected MS-DOS
version is running. SetVer merely fools those programs
into running by telling them what they want to hear.
SetVer is installed when you **boot** your computer by the
command *device=c:\dos\setver.exe*. (The MS-DOS Setup
program places this command in your **CONFIG.SYS** file
for you.) SETVER.EXE loads a version table into memory
that contains a list of programs and the MS-DOS version
that they require to run. When you run one of the programs in the table, SetVer supplies the program the
MS-DOS version number it needs.

Working with the SetVer Version Table

To display the SetVer version table, type *setver* at the command
prompt. To add or change an entry in the table, type *setver,* followed
by the name of the program you want to add to the table, followed by
the MS-DOS version number it needs, like this:

```
setver antique.exe 3.3
```

To delete an entry from the SetVer table, type *setver*, followed by the
name of the program you want to delete from the table, like this:

```
setver antique.exe
```

Save memory: Don't use SetVer

If you display the SetVer version table and discover you do not use any
of the programs it contains, you can save some memory by not loading
the SetVer device driver. Simply use the MS-DOS **Editor** to "comment
out" the *device=c:\dos\setver.exe* line in your CONFIG.SYS file by in-
serting **Rem** or a semicolon at the beginning of the line.

Share   The Share command installs a **memory-resident program** named SHARE.EXE that enables programs to share files. SHARE.EXE monitors access to your files and ensures that two programs do not attempt to modify a file at the same time. You can load SHARE.EXE by typing *share* at the command prompt, or you can insert the following command in your **CONFIG.SYS** file:

```
install=c:\dos\share.exe
```

Shell   The Shell command specifies the location of COMMAND.COM and the amount of memory set aside to store **environment variables.** You can use it only in **CONFIG.SYS**. The MS-DOS Setup program normally places COMMAND.COM in the **root directory** of your boot disk and sets aside 256 bytes of memory to hold environment variables. If your COMMAND.COM is located in the root directory of your boot disk, you won't need to use the Shell command unless you want to change the environment size. If COMMAND.COM is located in another directory (for example, the C:\DOS directory), you can use Shell in your CONFIG.SYS file to specify its location, like this:

```
shell=c:\dos\command.com
```

To change the environment size, add /E: and the environment size you want at the end of the line, like this:

```
shell=c:\dos\command.com  /e:512
```

Shift   The Shift command is used in **batch programs** to step through a series of replaceable **parameters** supplied on the command line. Each time the Shift command is executed, the first parameter in the series is thrown away and the second moves to the first position, the third to second, and so on. The following lines show how Shift works in a batch file:

```
:start
if "%1"=="" goto end
echo %1
shift
goto start
:end
```

In this example, the user can supply as many parameters as needed on the command line, and they will be displayed on the screen one by one, in order.

SMARTDrive   SMARTDrive is a program that speeds up disk access by setting aside a portion of memory to act as a "disk cache"—a place to hold a temporary copy of information recently read from a disk (called read caching) or information about to be written to a disk (called write caching). MS-DOS then retrieves this temporary copy from the cache instead of from the disk the next time you need the same information. Because MS-DOS can retrieve information from memory much faster than it can from a disk, you get your information much faster.

Starting SMARTDrive

To set up a disk cache, use the MS-DOS **Editor** to place the following
line in your **AUTOEXEC.BAT** file:

`c:\dos\smartdrv`

By default, MS-DOS sets up read caching on all disk drives on your
system and write caching on your hard drives. To add write caching on
specific drives, add the drive letter and a plus sign. To disable caching
on a specific drive, add the drive letter and a minus sign. For example,

`c:\dos\smartdrv c+ a- b-`

enables read and write caching on drive C, and disables all caching on
drives A and B.

Checking on SMARTDrive

After SMARTDrive is running, you can check on the size of the cache
and which drives are read cached and write cached by typing *smartdrv*
at the command prompt.

Using SMARTDrive Monitor with Windows

If you use Windows, you can run SmartDrive Monitor, a program that
displays information about your SMARTDrive caching. In addition to
showing the current SMARTDrive settings, SmartDrive Monitor con-
tinually updates its display to show how well your current settings
are working. To run SmartDrive Monitor, open Program Manager's File menu and
choose Run. Type *smartmon* and choose OK.

FastOpen; RAMDrive

Sort

The Sort command sorts lines of text into ascending order (A to Z, or numerically from lowest to highest). You can tell Sort to display the sorted result on the screen, send it to the printer, or save it in a file. You can also tell Sort to reverse the alphabetical order (Z to A) or to sort the text beginning at a specified column number, rather than at the beginning of the line.

Sorting a Text File

To sort a text file and display the result on the screen , type *sort* at the command prompt, followed by the < **redirection** symbol, followed by the name of the text file you want to sort. For example,

```
sort < list.txt
```

sorts the file LIST.TXT and displays the result on the screen. To save the sorted result in a file instead of displaying it, add the > redirection symbol and the name of the sorted file at the end of the command line, like this:

```
sort < list.txt > newlist.txt
```

To print the sorted result, add the > symbol but substitute *prn* for the sorted file name.

Customized Sorting

To sort in reverse order, from Z to A or numerically from highest to lowest, insert /R between *sort* and the < symbol, like this:

```
sort /r < list.txt > newlist.txt
```

To sort according to the text at a specified column number in each line, say column 25, insert /+ and the column number between *sort* and the < symbol, like this:

```
sort /+25 < list.txt > newlist.txt
```

Combining Sort with other commands

You can combine Sort with other commands using **piping** to achieve some pretty exotic results. For example, you can sort a directory listing by piping the **Dir** command to the Sort command, like this: *dir ¦ sort*. Or you can pipe sorted information from Sort to another command, such as **Find** or **More**, like this:

```
dir ¦ sort /r ¦ find "BAT"
```

This command sorts a directory listing in reverse order, and displays only lines containing "BAT." (A cynic might suggest that this could be more easily done by typing *dir *.bat /o–n*. But our convoluted version finds and correctly sorts *any* occurrence of BAT anywhere in the Dir output—not only in the filename extension.)

Stacks   The Stacks command is used in **CONFIG.SYS** to tell MS-DOS how much memory to set aside for its own temporary use. MS-DOS takes care of this for you during Setup, and you shouldn't need to use this command under most circumstances. If a program requires a particular Stacks setting, it will tell you how to change your CONFIG.SYS file.

Subdirectory   A subdirectory is a directory on a disk that is contained within another directory (called the **parent directory**)—like a manila folder contained within a hanging folder. In a sense, all directories are contained within a disk's **root directory** and are all subdirectories of the root directory.

Submenu   The Submenu command (MS-DOS version 6 only) can be used in a **multiple configuration CONFIG.SYS** file. The Submenu command creates and displays a second set of options to choose from after the user chooses a menu item during startup.

For example, the following line in your CONFIG.SYS file's [menu] block creates a submenu called *pointing_device* that appears when the user selects the startup menu item *graphics:*

```
submenu=pointing_device,graphics
```

You must, of course, also add a block with the header [pointing_device] that contains one or more menu items so that the user has something from which to choose.

🐾 **[Menu] Header; MenuItem**

Subst   The Subst command lets you treat a directory as if it were a separate disk drive. Subst is a handy way to create a shortcut name for a long or complicated **pathname**. For example, you might want a short way to refer to the C:\TRAVEL\SAFARI\CLIPART\ANIMAL\BIGCATS directory. Subst provides the shortcut. Place the following line in your AUTOEXEC.BAT file:

```
subst z: c:\travel\safari\clipart\animal\bigcats
```

You can now find that picture of the leopard by typing *dir z:*. You can use any drive letter you want, but the letter must be within the range specified by the **LastDrive** command in your **CONFIG.SYS** file.

To delete the drive substitution when you no longer need it, simply remove the line from your **AUTOEXEC.BAT** file and reboot. Or, to delete the substitution for the current session, include the drive letter and /D. For example, to cancel the substitution made in the example above, type *subst z: /d* at the command prompt. You can also check on which substitutions are in effect by typing *subst* at the command prompt.

Supplemental Disk   The Supplemental Disk includes **MS-DOS Shell** and some utilities for people with disabilities and for creating a bootable **DoubleSpace** floppy disk, as well as some totally useless utilities and obsolete programs from earlier MS-DOS versions. The disk is available at no charge from Microsoft's CompuServe forum and is included with the **Resource Kit**. You can also order it for a nominal charge directly from Microsoft: Call Microsoft Sales at (800) 426-9400 (U.S.) or (800) 563-9048 (Canada).

Sys   The Sys command copies the MS-DOS operating system files from one disk to another, making the second disk "bootable." Sys copies COMMAND.COM and the hidden files IO.SYS, MSDOS.SYS, and (if you use DoubleSpace) DBLSPACE.BIN. To copy the system files from the **current drive** to a **floppy disk**, simply type *sys* followed by the destination drive letter, like this:

```
sys a:
```

⁘ **Attrib; File Attributes; Format**

System File Attribute   ⁘ **Attrib; File Attributes**

Task Swapper   Task Swapper is a feature of **MS-DOS Shell** that lets you start several programs and switch among them with just a few keystrokes. To use Task Swapper, choose Enable Task Swapper from MS-DOS Shell's Options menu. An Active Task List pane opens to the right of the Program List. Although Task Swapper lets you switch to another program without quitting the current program, only the displayed program is running; all other programs in the Active Task List are suspended.

Starting Multiple Programs

To start multiple programs from MS-DOS Shell, select each program from the File List or Program List and press Shift+Enter. Or, press and hold the Shift key while double-clicking each program name. Each program you select is added to the Active Task List.

continues

Task Swapper *(continued)*

Switching Among Programs

- To go to a program from MS-DOS Shell, select its name in the Active Task List and press Enter. Or, double-click its name.

- To leave a program and return to MS-DOS Shell, press Ctrl+Esc.

- To go directly from one program to the next in the Active Task List without returning to MS-DOS Shell, press Alt+Esc; to go to the previous program in the Active Task List, press Shift+Alt+Esc.

- To choose among any of the programs in the Active Task List without returning to MS-DOS Shell, hold down the Alt key and press Tab repeatedly until the name of the program you want is displayed, and then release the Alt key. To cycle backward through the Active Task List, hold down the Alt key and press Shift+Tab.

Time   The Time command lets you display and change the time in your computer's clock. Type *time* at the command prompt and MS-DOS displays the current time with a prompt for you to enter a new time.

```
Current time is 1:09:45.12p
Enter new time:
```

To leave the time as it is, simply press Enter. To change the time, type a new value. Separate the hours, minutes, and seconds with colons (:), and add an *a* or *p* at the end for *am* or *pm*.

"Reveille is at 0530, soldier"

By default, MS-DOS displays times in the 12-hour format, like this: 4:59:00.00p. If you prefer to see 24-hour format (e.g., 16:59:00) or a different separator (a period or a comma), add a command like this to your **CONFIG.SYS** file:

```
country=033,,c:\dos\country.sys
```

Replace 033 with the code for a country that uses the time format you want. A list of countries, their codes, and the date and time format is in online **Help** for the Country command.

Date

Tree   The Tree command displays a map of a disk's
subdirectories in a tree structure, like this:

To use the Tree command, type *tree* at the command
prompt, followed by the drive and path for which you
want to see the tree. If you don't include a drive or path,
MS-DOS displays the tree for the **current drive** and
starting from the **current directory**. To display the files in
each directory, add /F to the Tree command, like this:

    tree /f

Printing the Tree Structure

You can print a copy of your disk's directory tree by using **redirection**
to send the output of the Tree command to your printer. Append > *prn*
to the Tree command, like this: *tree > prn*.

If your printer spews unusual characters instead of graceful branch
lines, include the /A switch, like this: *tree /a > prn*.

Type

The Type command displays the contents of a text file on screen. The file must be a plain text file, like those you can create or edit with MS-DOS **Editor.** Type cannot properly display the contents of formatted word processor files, program files, or graphic files.

To use Type, enter *type* at the command prompt followed by a space and the **filename** you want to see. For example,

```
type readme.txt
```

displays the contents of the file README.TXT.

Hold that tiger

Type can be a little overzealous in displaying your file. Type does not pause after each screenful of information, and a large file's contents can easily fly by on the screen before you get a chance to look at it. Here are two tips you can use to tame the Type command:

- Press Ctrl+S to pause the display at any point. To resume, press any key.

- Use **piping** to send Type's output to the **More** command, like this: *type readme.txt | more.* More displays just one screenful at a time, politely waiting for you to press a key before displaying the next screenful.

UMB

A UMB, an acronym for "Upper Memory Block," is an area in your computer's **memory** into which MS-DOS can load **device drivers** and **memory-resident programs,** such as **Doskey.** To use UMBs, your computer must have a 386, 486, or Pentium processor, and you must use a memory management program such as **EMM386.EXE.**

Undelete

The Undelete command restores deleted files—provided MS-DOS has not reused the space formerly occupied by the deleted file. For the best chance of res ing a deleted file, use Undelete as soon as possible, pre ably before writing any other information to the disk.

Using Undelete

To use Undelete, follow these steps:

1 Change to the directory that contained the file(s) before deleti

2 Type *undelete* at the command prompt.

3 Undelete displays all the deleted files in the current directory, ginning with the most recently deleted. After each file, Undel stops and asks whether you want to undelete it. If you do, pre

4 If you did not have **Delete Sentry** or **Delete Tracker** enable when the file was deleted, Undelete asks you to supply the fi character in the **filename**. Type a character.

Total recall

You can tell Undelete to restore all deleted files without stopping to ask about each one by adding /ALL to the command line, like this: *undelete /a* this case, Undelete replaces the first character in the deleted filename with t symbol. When all the files have been restored, you can use the **Ren** command restore their rightful names.

con

Undelete *(continued)*

Using Undelete for Windows

MS-DOS also includes a Windows-based version of Undelete. Unlike the MS-DOS—based version, Undelete for Windows lets you change directories, sort the deleted files, and search for a deleted file by name, location, or content. To use Undelete for Windows, follow these steps:

1 Double-click the Undelete icon in the **Microsoft Tools program group.**

2 Click the Drive/Dir button to display the Change Drive and Directory dialog box. Type the **pathname** for the directory that contained the file(s) before deletion and click OK.

3 Undelete displays a list of deleted files in the current directory. Click the name of each file you want to undelete, or use the direction keys to move the dotted line and press Spacebar to highlight a filename.

4 Click the Undelete button to undelete the selected files.

5 If you did not have Delete Sentry or Delete Tracker enabled when the file was deleted, Undelete asks you to supply the first character in the filename. Type a character and click OK.

Del

Unformat The Unformat command helps you recover from an accidental reformatting of either a **floppy disk** or your hard disk. Unformat can be a lifesaver when you need it, but it has some limitations:

- Unformat will not work if you used the /U switch when you formatted the disk.

- Unformat cannot recover fragmented files (files with pieces stored in different places on the disk).

- Unformat cannot recover any files after you write any new files to the disk.

To recover an accidentally formatted floppy disk in drive A, for example, type *unformat a:* and follow the directions that appear on the screen.

To recover an accidentally formatted hard disk, you must have a floppy disk containing the MS-DOS system files and the Unformat program, UNFORMAT.COM. Insert this system disk in drive A and reboot your computer. Then type *unformat c:* and follow the directions that appear on the screen.

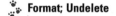 **Format; Undelete**

Uninstall To uninstall an MS-DOS upgrade and return to an earlier version, place the Uninstall disk that you created in the upgrade process in drive A, restart your computer, and follow the instructions that appear on the screen.

Ver   The Ver command reports which version of MS-DOS you are using.

Getting the latest and greatest

If Ver tells you that you have MS-DOS Version 6.0, you should consider upgrading to version 6.2. It offers several enhancements and it's cheap! This "step-up" is available for downloading from CompuServe and other online services, or you can purchase it for a nominal fee from your local software reseller.

Verify   The Verify command instructs MS-DOS to double check for accuracy each time it writes information to disk. Although this sounds like a good idea, you pay a steep price: Verify slows down disk writes considerably. Moreover, Verify is normally unnecessary. (Writing to disk is one of MS-DOS's main purposes for being, and it does so 99.99% of the time quite accurately, thank you.)

But if you like to wear suspenders along with a belt, you can turn verify on by typing *verify on* at the command prompt or by placing the same line in your **AUTOEXEC.BAT** file.

To turn verify off, type *verify off*. If you type *verify* by itself at the command prompt, MS-DOS tells you whether verify is on or off.

Virus   ⁖ **Anti-Virus; VSafe**

Vol

The Vol command displays a disk's **volume label.** It is similar to the **Label** command except that Vol does not let you change the label, just display it.

To use the Vol command, type *vol* at the command prompt followed by the drive letter containing the disk. For example,

```
vol a:
```

displays the volume label for the disk in drive A.

Volume Label

A volume label is an optional name you give to a disk when it is formatted. The volume label appears at the top of the disk's directory listing.

Displaying the volume label—**Vol**

Changing or deleting a volume label—**Label**

VSafe

The VSafe command loads the VSafe program into **memory,** where it watches for activities that might signal the presence of a virus. To start VSafe, simply type *vsafe* at the command prompt.

VSafe has a number of options that you can use to customize it to provide the level of virus protection you want. Simply add the option or options you want with a plus or minus sign to turn the option on or off, like this:

```
vsafe /8+ /4-
```

continues

VSafe *(continued)*

Option	Default	Description
/1	On	Warns when a hard disk is about to be formatted
/2	Off	Warns when a program tries to stay in memory
/3	Off	Prevents all programs from writing to disk
/4	On	Checks all executable files for viruses before running them
/5	On	Checks the boot sector of all disks for viruses
/6	On	Warns when a program tries to write to the boot sector of your hard disk
/7	Off	Warns when a program tries to write to the boot sector of a floppy disk
/8	Off	Warns when a program tries to modify an executable file

🐾 **Anti-Virus**

Wildcard   A wildcard is a special symbol you can use to specify multiple files with certain MS-DOS commands. MS-DOS recognizes two wildcards: * and ?.

The asterisk (*) represents a group of characters and is typically used to represent any **filename** or extension. For example, *.* means all files; *.txt means all files with the extension TXT. You can also use it to represent the last part of a filename. For example, 93*.d* specifies all files that have names beginning with "93" and an extension that begins with d.

The question mark (?) stands for just one character in a filename or extension. For example, *?ed.txt* includes the files TED.TXT, NED.TXT, RED.TXT, and so on. You can use more than one question mark, such as *??e?.txt*, to include all TXT files with four-character filenames with *e* as the third letter.

You can also combine asterisks and question marks to get as general or specific as you need. For example, *?e?.** includes all three-character filenames with *e* as the second letter and any extension.

The following examples show how wildcard characters can be used with the **Dir** command to limit the list of files.

```
C:\>dir /b /o
DB-0510.DOC
DB-0517.DOC
DB-0804.DOC
HOBGOBLN.DOC
PM-0824.DOC
PM-0825.DOC
SMART.TXT
SQ&A.TXT
SYSADMIN.WRI
```
Without a **file specification**, Dir shows all files in the **current directory**. (The /B switch produces a "bare" filename-only list; /O sorts the names alphabetically.)

```
C:\>dir /b /o s*.*
SMART.TXT
SQ&A.TXT
SYSADMIN.WRI
```
Only filenames that start with *S* are displayed with this file specification.

```
C:\>dir /b /o ??-08*.*
DB-0804.DOC
PM-0824.DOC
PM-0825.DOC
```
This file specification includes letters written in August—those with "-08" following two other characters.

Oh, my stars!

Be careful when using wildcards for deleting. A command such as *del *.** will delete all the files in your current directory!

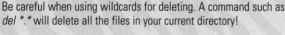

WINA20.386   This file, which MS-DOS Setup places in the **root directory** of drive C, is a device driver for Windows 3.0. You need it only if you run Windows version 3.0 in 386 Enhanced mode. If you don't use Windows or you have a more recent Windows version (such as Windows version 3.1, Windows for Workgroups, or Windows NT), you can delete the WINA20.386 file. Because it has the read-only **file attribute** set, you must first use **Attrib** to change the attribute, and then use **Del** to erase the file.

Windows-Based Application   A Windows-based application is a program that requires Microsoft Windows to run. If you type the name of a Windows-based application's executable file at the command prompt, the program displays this message:

```
This program requires Microsoft Windows.
```

If you have Windows on your computer, type *win* to start Windows, and then start the Windows-based application.

XCopy   The XCopy command, short for "eXtended Copy," is similar to the **Copy** command, but gives you a few more options. With XCopy, you can:

- Copy entire directories and subdirectories as well as individual files

- Copy only files created or modified after a certain date

- Have XCopy ask you before copying each file

Copying Directories

The /S switch tells XCopy to copy subdirectories as well as files. For example, to copy all the files and subdirectories in the current directory to the disk in drive A, type:

```
xcopy *.* a: /s
```

This command copies all files and non-empty subdirectories. To copy the entire tree structure within the current directory, including empty directories, type:

```
xcopy *.* a: /s /e
```

Specifying a Date for Files to Copy

To copy only files created or modified after a specific date, use XCopy with the /D:*date* switch. For example, to copy all DOC files in the current directory with dates after December 31, 1993, to the disk in drive A, type:

```
xcopy *.doc a: /d:12-31-1993
```

Asking Before Copying

To have XCopy prompt you before copying each file, use the /P switch, like this:

```
xcopy *.doc a: /p
```

XMS Memory 🐾 Memory

TROUBLE-SHOOTING

Got a problem? Starting on the next page are solutions to the problems that can plague users of MS-DOS. You'll be on your way—and safely out of danger—in no time.

CONFIGURATION AND STARTUP

Your Computer Stops Running and Won't Restart

If your computer stops running, you'll need to "reboot" (restart) it. Many times this solves the problem and you can continue working. If you cannot successfully restart your computer, try the solutions below.

Do an interactive boot

1 Press Ctrl+Alt+Del. (If your computer does not respond, turn the power off, wait at least 15 seconds, and then turn the power back on.)

2 When the "Starting MS-DOS..." message appears, press F8. MS-DOS then prompts for each line in the CONFIG.SYS and AUTOEXEC.BAT files, asking whether the line should be executed.

3 Watch for any error messages as each line is executed. Correct any errors and reboot your computer again.

Bypass CONFIG.SYS and AUTOEXEC.BAT completely

1 Press Ctrl+Alt+Del. (If your computer does not respond, turn the power off, wait at least 15 seconds, and then turn the power back on.)

2 When the "Starting MS-DOS..." message appears, press F5. Your computer will bypass CONFIG.SYS and AUTOEXEC.BAT and start with a basic configuration.

Booting without device drivers

A minimal configuration does not load installable device drivers; as a result, some devices (such as the mouse) might not function. If you use a third-party disk-compression program (such as Stacker), you should use the F8 key (instead of F5) during startup so that you can execute the commands necessary to allow any compressed drives to be read when you're finished rebooting. (DoubleSpace loads its drivers even if you press F5; if you want to boot without DoubleSpace for some reason, press Ctrl+F5 to bypass CONFIG.SYS and AUTOEXEC.BAT altogether, or Ctrl+F8 for an interactive boot without DoubleSpace.)

Boot; AUTOEXEC.BAT; CONFIG.SYS

Your System Doesn't Have the Windows-Based Utilities

MS-DOS version 6 includes Windows-based versions of Microsoft Backup, Microsoft Anti-Virus, and Microsoft Undelete. You can install these programs during Setup. However, if you didn't, you can install them any time.

Use Setup /E

1 Insert Setup Disk 1 in your floppy disk drive.
2 At the command prompt, type *a:setup /e* and press Enter.

 Anti-Virus; Backup; Undelete; Windows-Based Application

MEMORY

You Can't Run Programs Because There Isn't Enough Memory

Some programs don't run properly or make certain features unavailable if your computer doesn't have enough free conventional memory. Other programs won't even start.

Use MemMaker

You can optimize your computer's memory use automatically by running the MemMaker program. MemMaker works on 386, 486, and Pentium computer systems only; it does not work on 80286 or 8088 systems. And it works only with the MS-DOS HIMEM.SYS and EMM386.EXE memory-management utilities; it does not work with third-party utilities, such as QEMM and 386MAX.

MemMaker reviews your CONFIG.SYS and AUTOEXEC.BAT files and then optimizes them by loading installable device drivers and memory-resident programs into upper memory, thereby making more conventional memory available for programs.

continues

You Can't Run Programs... *(continued)*

1 Before you run MemMaker, verify that all device drivers are being loaded properly and that any hardware they control is also functioning correctly.

2 To run MemMaker, type *memmaker* at the command prompt.

3 Follow the instructions on the screen. When asked, choose either Express Setup or Custom Setup. We recommend initially using the Express Setup; you can always run the Custom Setup later if necessary.

4 MemMaker reboots your machine twice while it determines the optimal configuration. When it has chosen a configuration, a screen reports how much memory was available before you ran MemMaker and how much is available now.

5 If the displayed memory is not what you expect or need, press Esc to undo changes made by MemMaker.

6 If you accepted the changes made by MemMaker and now want to undo them, type *memmaker /undo* at the command prompt.

If MemMaker fails you

MemMaker tries to use upper memory locations that it determines are free. If your machine hangs, note any error messages that are displayed, and then restart your computer. MemMaker detects that your computer is being restarted before the optimization is complete and displays a screen listing possible reasons for the interruption and instructions for resuming or quitting the optimization. Accept the default options to continue.

Memory; MemMaker; CONFIG.SYS; AUTOEXEC.BAT; HIMEM.SYS; EMM386.EXE; Device Driver; Memory-Resident Programs; DeviceHigh; LoadHigh

MemMaker Won't Optimize Multiple Configurations

MemMaker views the CONFIG.SYS and AUTOEXEC.BAT files as a single unit. Therefore, MemMaker cannot optimize CONFIG.SYS and AUTOEXEC.BAT files that use multiple configuration commands. To optimize multiple configurations using MemMaker, you must have separate configuration files for each item on your multiple configuration menu, and run MemMaker on each set of files. This is a complex process and should be approached with caution. You may want to copy these files onto a floppy disk first—just in case.

MemMaker; CONFIG.SYS; AUTOEXEC.BAT; Multiple Configurations

After Running MemMaker, Some Programs and Device Drivers Won't Run Properly

MemMaker is very clever about loading memory-resident programs and installable device drivers into unused sections of memory. Unfortunately, some older programs and device drivers are just not designed to be loaded into upper memory.

Load the program or driver into conventional memory

If the device driver is being loaded from the CONFIG.SYS file with a DeviceHigh command, follow these steps:

1 Use Editor to load CONFIG.SYS.

2 Change the line for the device driver to read "device=" instead of "devicehigh=." Delete everything between the equal sign and the file specification for the driver. (This is typically a /L switch followed by some numbers.)

3 Save the changes to CONFIG.SYS.

4 Restart your computer.

continues

After Running MemMaker, Some Programs... *(continued)*

If the program is being loaded in the AUTOEXEC.BAT file, follow these steps:

1 Use Editor to load AUTOEXEC.BAT.

2 Delete the word "loadhigh" and all text before the file specification for the program.

3 Save the changes to AUTOEXEC.BAT.

4 Restart your computer.

Memory; Device Driver; Device; DeviceHigh; LoadHigh; MemMaker

Files and Disks

MS-DOS Doesn't Automatically Recognize a DoubleSpace-Compressed Floppy Disk When You Insert It

If you use MS-DOS version 6.0, DoubleSpace does not automatically "mount" a disk when you insert it in the drive. Instead, the disk's directory lists only one file: READTHIS.TXT. Although the Automount feature in version 6.2 automatically detects and mounts compressed floppies, Automount might not be enabled, or you might need to increase the number of drive letters.

Mount the disk manually

At the command prompt, type *dblspace /mount a:* or *dblspace /mount b:*.

If this command reports that you don't have any available drive letters, follow these steps:

1 At the command prompt, type *dblspace*.

2 Choose the Options command from the Tools menu.

3 Select a higher letter (that is, one closer to the end of the alphabet) in the Last Drive Reserved for DoubleSpace's Use box. Choose OK.

4 Choose Mount from the Drive menu to mount the disk.

5 Choose Exit from the Drive menu to quit the DoubleSpace program.

Upgrade to MS-DOS version 6.2

Purchase and install the MS-DOS 6.2 Step-Up. It's inexpensive, and thereafter you can use compressed floppy disks without messing around with "mount" commands.

Be sure Automount is enabled

1 At the command prompt, type *dblspace*.

2 Choose the Options command from the Tools menu.

3 Select Enable Automount and choose OK.

4 Choose Exit from the Drive menu to quit the DoubleSpace program.

🐾 **DoubleSpace; Automount; Ver**

Backup Won't Restore Files Backed Up Using an Earlier Version of MS-DOS

The version of Microsoft Backup included with MS-DOS version 6 cannot read backup files made with the Backup command included with MS-DOS versions 5 and earlier. Don't fret; your files are still recoverable.

Use the Restore command

1 Insert the disk that contains the backed-up files in drive A or B.

2 To restore all the files to drive C, type the following at the command prompt:

```
restore a: c:\*.* /s
```
or
```
restore b: c:\*.* /s
```

3 Follow the instructions on the screen to complete the restore procedure.

🐾 **Restore; Backup**

You Can't Find a File

Files can be lost for many reasons. Most of the time, you can't find a file because you can't remember where it is on your hard disk, or you deleted it—either on purpose or by accident.

Use Dir to find a lost file that still exists on your hard disk

Add the /S (subdirectory) switch to the Dir command. For example, to find the file MISSING.TXT, type *dir \missing.txt /s*. MS-DOS searches each directory and displays the filename if it finds it.

Use Undelete to find a lost file that has been deleted

More often than you'd probably like to admit, files are lost because they have been deleted from your hard disk. Many times you'll delete a file or two by accident. (A select few have even said good-bye to entire directories!) Just as often, you're likely to delete files and directories on purpose, thinking you'll never use them again or because you're trying to recover much-needed disk space.

Not to worry (most of the time)! Undelete can assist you in recovering "lost" files. Your success in recovery depends on what shape the deleted file is in (which usually depends on how long ago it was deleted because a deleted file's space can be overwritten when you copy other files onto the disk) and whether you use Delete Sentry, Delete Tracker, or standard undelete protection.

1 Change to the directory where the file was located.

2 Type *undelete* and follow the on-screen instructions.

Dir; Undelete; Delete Sentry; Delete Tracker

All Files on Your Current Drive Were Deleted When You Used the Command "DelTree *.* /Y"

The DelTree command allows you to delete entire directories—including all files and subdirectories—with one command. Before DelTree begins deleting, it issues a message asking you to verify that you want to delete all the files and directories from the current drive. However, the /Y parameter bypasses this verification message.

The best way to avoid making this mistake is to not use potentially dangerous commands such as DelTree unless absolutely necessary.

❖ DelTree

ChkDsk Reports Lost Allocation Units

Lost allocation units and other errors reported by ChkDsk indicate a mismatch between the directory of files maintained by MS-DOS and the actual files on the disk. ChkDsk can convert these unidentified pieces of files into files that you can examine (and usually throw away, which makes the space available for use again).

Use the /F parameter with ChkDsk

1 At the command prompt, type *chkdsk /f.*

2 ChkDsk asks if you want to convert the lost allocation units to files. If you want to see what the lost allocation units contain, type *y.* (If you know you don't want to look at these files, type *n* and ChkDsk deletes the lost allocation units, freeing up disk space.)

3 ChkDsk creates files in the root directory. These files have the extension CHK and have filenames such as FILE0000.CHK. You can use Type or Editor to look at them (they usually contain "garbage"), and then delete the ones you don't want.

❖ ChkDsk; ScanDisk

MS-DOS Error Messages

Access denied

The file you are attempting to use is unavailable. It is either being used by another user or another application, or it has the read-only attribute set.

Remove the read-only attribute

Use the Attrib command to change the attribute. If the file you tried to access when you received the error is called TIME.TXT, for example, type *attrib -r time.txt* at the command prompt.

File Attributes; Attrib

Bad command or file name

This message appears when you type something that MS-DOS doesn't recognize. You might be typing an MS-DOS command, or a command to start a program. Here are the most common reasons for getting this message:

- You typed the command wrong; that is, you misspelled it.

- The command or executable file (program or batch) is not in the current directory, and the directory where the command resides is not in your search path.

When you type a command or program name, MS-DOS first looks in the current directory for the corresponding filename. For example, typing *bingo* might start your favorite BINGO game. (The actual filename might be BINGO.EXE.) If it can't be found in the current directory, then MS-DOS looks in the directories specified in your Path statement (if you've entered one; it's usually in your AUTOEXEC.BAT file). If BINGO.EXE still can't be found, the "Bad command or filename" message is displayed.

Add the directory to your Path statement

1 Use Editor to open AUTOEXEC.BAT.

2 Add the pathname (drive and directory path) for the directory that contains the program file to the end of the Path command. Be sure a semicolon separates the pathname from the preceding one. For example, after you add the C:\GAMES\BINGO directory to the search path, the Path command might look like this:

```
PATH C:\DOS;C:\GAMES\BINGO
```

3 Save the changes to AUTOEXEC.BAT and exit Editor.

4 Restart your computer.

Include the pathname with the command

If you don't want to add the program's directory to your search path, you can include the pathname as part of the file specification when you run the command. For example, typing *games\bingo\bingo* tells MS-DOS to look for the BINGO program in the \GAMES\BINGO directory.

Path; Pathname

Bad or missing command interpreter

MS-DOS cannot find the COMMAND.COM file. This might happen if you are restarting your computer with a basic configuration (bypassing CONFIG.SYS and AUTOXEC.BAT).

Type the full path

When MS-DOS prompts you to specify the path to the COMMAND.COM file, type the full path to the file (for example, C:\DOS\COMMAND.COM).

Boot; Pathname

DMA buffer size too small

If you have installed Windows or the EMM386 device driver on your computer, this message might appear when you run the Backup compatibility test or start a backup.

Increase the size of the DMA buffer

1 Open the SYSTEM.INI file—located in your Windows directory—using a text editor such as Notepad or MS-DOS Editor.

2 Find the [386Enh] section of SYSTEM.INI and add the following line:

```
dmabuffersize=32
```

3 Save the changes to SYSTEM.INI.

4 Exit Windows.

5 Restart Windows.

EMS page frame not found *or* Expanded memory not available

This message appears when you use a program that requires expanded memory and your configuration is set up to disable expanded memory.

Run MemMaker

When MemMaker asks you if you use any programs that require expanded memory, choose Yes.

 MemMaker

DMA SIZE=32
BUFFER
166

When you start your computer, either by turning on the power or restarting it after the power is on, it first goes through a series of diagnostic tests and then looks for a "bootable" disk—one with operating system files on it. Most systems look first at drive A; if you have a "non-system" disk in drive A (one that is not bootable because it doesn't have operating system files on it), you'll get this message.

Remove the floppy disk

Remove the disk from drive A (or simply open the drive door) and press any key to continue booting your system.

Be sure the floppy disk has system files

If you intended to boot from drive A and you got this message, then you need to replace the disk in drive A with one that is bootable. It should have (at the very least) COMMAND.COM plus the hidden files MSDOS.SYS and IO.SYS on the disk for it to be considered bootable. To create a bootable disk, type *sys a:* at the command prompt.

Boot; Sys

Not ready reading
drive A
Abort, Retry, Fail?

The drive door may not be closed properly, or the disk may not be inserted properly in the disk drive.

Reinsert the disk

1 Be sure the disk is inserted label-side up.

2 Close the drive door, making sure the disk clicks into the disk drive.

3 Press R for Retry.

continues

Not ready reading drive A... *(continued)*

Working with finicky drives

Sometimes it helps to open the drive door, press R for Retry and then slowly close the drive door as the disk drive starts to spin (the drive light comes on). This may seat the disk properly as it spins.

Out of environment space

There is insufficient environment space to hold the current environment variable definition.

Increase the environment space

1 Use Editor to open CONFIG.SYS.

2 Include a Shell command that specifies COMMAND.COM as the shell and includes the /E parameter to increase the environment size. For example, /E:1024 sets an environment space of 1024 bytes, like this:

```
shell=command.com /e:1024 /p
```

Out of memory

If you are getting out of memory messages while running programs such as Anti-Virus, Backup, or Undelete, you can make more memory available by one of the following methods:

• Run MemMaker to "tune up" your CONFIG.SYS and AUTOEXEC.BAT files.

• Do an interactive boot—as described at the beginning of the Troubleshooting section—to prevent selected programs from loading, thus freeing up memory.

 **MemMaker; Boot**

QUICK REFERENCE

Any time you explore some exotic location, you're bound to see flora and fauna you can't identify. To make sure you can identify the commands and toolbar buttons you see in MS-DOS, the Quick Reference describes these items in systematic detail.

MENU, FUNCTION KEY, AND BUTTON GUIDE

You carry out most MS-DOS commands by typing a command at the command prompt—which promptly returns when the command is finished. A few MS-DOS commands open into a full screen that includes toolbars and drop-down menus. They're all described here.

To drop down a menu, hold down the Alt key and press the underlined or highlighted letter of the menu you want. Then, to choose a command, simply press its underlined or highlighted letter. You can also use a mouse to choose commands: Click the menu name to drop down the menu, and then click a command name.

Anti-Virus for MS-DOS

Menu Options

Detect	Scans the current work drive for known viruses (ones that are in the virus list); if any viruses are detected, you can clean or delete the infected file, continue without cleaning, or stop scanning
Detect & Clean	Scans the current work drive and removes known viruses (ones that are in the virus list) from your system
Select new drive	Displays the drive line so you can select a different drive to scan and/or clean
Options	Allows you to configure Anti-Virus's options for your specific needs; options can be saved when you exit the program
Exit	Exits Anti-Virus; if you check Save Configuration, any changes you have made to the program's configuration are saved

Function Keys

F1 Help	Displays Help for the current selection
F2 Drive	Displays the drive line so you can select a different drive to scan and/or clean
F3 Exit	Stops the current operation or exits the program

F4 Detect Scans the current work drive for viruses; if any viruses are detected, you can clean or delete the infected file, continue without cleaning, or stop scanning

F5 Clean Scans the current work drive for viruses; if a virus is detected, the infected file is cleaned and the scan continues to the next file

F7 Delete Deletes CHKLIST.MS checklist files (a list of executable files stored to protect against known viruses)

F8 Options Allows you to configure the program to your specific needs; options can be saved when you exit the program

F9 List Displays a list of all the viruses recognized by Anti-Virus; you can search for a specific virus, or display or print information about a selected virus

Anti-Virus for Windows

Scan Menu

Detect Scans the selected drives for known viruses (ones that are in the virus list); if any viruses are detected, you can clean or delete the infected file, continue without cleaning, or stop scanning

Clean Scans the selected drives and removes known viruses (ones that are in the virus list) from your system

Delete CHKLST files Deletes CHKLIST.MS checklist files (a list of executable files stored to protect against known viruses)

Virus List Displays a list of all the viruses recognized by Anti-Virus; you can search for a specific virus, or display or print information about a selected virus

Exit Anti-Virus Exits Anti-Virus for Windows; if you have selected the Save Settings On Exit option, any changes you have made to the program's configuration are saved

continues

Anti-Virus for Windows *(continued)*

Options Menu

Set Options...	Configures Anti-Virus's options for your specific needs; options can be saved when you exit the program
Save Settings on Exit	Check this option to save your current configuration settings when you exit Anti-Virus

Help Menu

Index	Displays a list of topics for Anti-Virus
Keyboard	Displays a list of keyboard keys and their functions for Anti-Virus
Glossary	Displays a list of Anti-Virus terms; click a term to see its meaning
Using Help	Displays a list of topics about how to use the Windows Help facility
About Anti-Virus...	Displays version and copyright information about Anti-Virus

Backup

Buttons

Button	Description
Backup	Creates a backup set of files from your hard disk
Compare	Verifies that a backup set contains exact copies of the files you backed up from your hard disk
Restore	Copies files from the backup set onto your hard disk

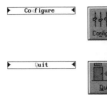		Configures Backup for your specific needs and preferences
		Exits Backup; optionally saves the current configuration and settings to the current setup file

File Menu

Open Setup...	Opens a different setup file
Save Setup	Saves the current settings to the current setup file
Save Setup **A**s...	Saves the current settings to a different setup file
Delete Setup...	Deletes one or more setup files
Print	Prints the current setup file
P**r**inter Setup...	Selects a printer and sets available options
E**x**it	Exits Backup; optionally saves the current configuration and settings to the current setup file

Numbered File menu commands

Backup for Windows displays a list of the five most recently used setup files; select one to open it immediately.

Catalog Menu   (Backup for Windows only)

Load...	Selects a catalog from which you can select files to compare or restore
Retrieve...	Retrieves the backup catalog directly from the backup set and copies it to your hard disk
Re**b**uild...	Rebuilds a catalog directly from the backup set if part of the backup set is missing
Delete...	Deletes catalogs that are no longer needed on your hard disk

continues

Backup *(continued)*

Help Menu

Index	Displays a list of Help topics from which to choose
Keyboard	Displays help on using the keyboard and mouse with Backup
Basic Skills	Displays a summary of steps to use each Backup function
Backup	Displays a step-by-step overview of the Backup function
Compare	Displays a step-by-step overview of the Compare function
Restore	Displays a step-by-step overview of the Restore function
Configure	Displays an overview of the Configure function
Glossary	Displays a list of Backup terms; select a term to see its definition
Using Help	Displays a list of topics about how to use the Backup Help facility
About Backup...	Displays version and copyright information about Backup; Backup for Windows also identifies which Windows operating mode your system is using and how much memory is available

Defrag

Optimize Menu

Begin optimization	Starts "defragging" (optimizing) the selected drive
Drive...	Selects a drive to optimize
Optimization Method...	Selects between "full" optimization (which is more effective) and "files only" (which is faster)
File sort...	Selects order of files and directories on the optimized drive

Map legend...	Explains the symbols used in the Defrag screen
About Defrag...	Displays copyright information about Defrag
eXit	Quits Defrag

DoubleSpace

Drive Menu

Info...	Displays information about the selected DoubleSpace drive
Change Size...	Changes the size of a compressed drive
Change Ratio...	Changes the compression ratio used in free-space estimates
Mount...	Assigns a drive letter to a compressed volume file
Unmount...	Disassociates a drive letter and a compressed volume file
Format...	Erases all files on a compressed drive
Delete...	Deletes a compressed drive and all the files it contains, restoring the space to normal, uncompressed disk space
Exit	Quits the DoubleSpace program

Compress Menu

Existing Drive...	Converts an existing drive to a compressed drive
Create New Drive...	Creates a new compressed drive using only the free space on an existing drive

continues

DoubleSpace *(continued)*

Tools Menu

Defragment...	Reorganizes the files on a compressed drive to consolidate its free space
Uncompress...	Converts a DoubleSpace drive to a normal, uncompressed drive
Chkdsk...	Checks a compressed drive and corrects errors
Options...	Sets drive letter, Automount, and DoubleGuard options

Help Menu

Contents	Displays the table of contents for DoubleSpace help
Index	Displays the index for DoubleSpace help
About...	Displays DoubleSpace version and copyright information

Editor

File Menu

New	Clears the screen, which is used to create a new document
Open...	Opens an existing document
Save	Saves the current version of a document under the same name
Save **A**s...	Saves the current version of a document under a different name
Print...	Prints all or part of a document
E**x**it	Exits Editor

Edit Menu

Cut   Deletes selected text and places it on the Clipboard

Copy   Copies selected text and places it on the Clipboard

Paste   Inserts text from the Clipboard into your document at the current cursor position

Clear   Deletes selected text without placing it on the Clipboard

Search Menu

Find...   Searches for a text string

Repeat Last Find   Repeats the search performed by the most recent Find or Change command

Change...   Searches for a text string and replaces it with another text string

Options Menu

Display...   Controls screen settings, which are saved when you exit Editor

Help Path...   Changes the directory where Editor Help is located

Help Menu

Getting Started   Displays a list of topics that explain how to use Editor

Keyboard   Displays help topics that explain how to navigate and edit text in Editor

About...   Displays version and copyright information about Editor

MSD

File Menu

Find File...	Locates and views files
Print Report...	Prints a report to a printer or a file
Startup and INI files	Displays the selected file
E**x**it	Exits MSD

Utilities Menu

Memory Block Display...	Displays allocated memory for devices and programs currently being used on a visual memory map
Memory **B**rowser...	Searches for key words in ROM areas
Insert Command...	Inserts common commands in system files
Test Printer...	Tests your printer connection
Black & **W**hite	Toggles the screen between color and monochrome (black and white)

Help Menu

About...	Displays version and copyright information about MSD

MS-DOS Help

File Menu

Print...	Prints the current topic to a printer or a file
E**x**it	Exits Help

Search Menu

Find...   Searches for text

Repeat Last Find   Repeats the search performed by the most recent Find command

Help Menu

How to Use MS-DOS Help   Explains how to navigate the help system

About...   Displays version and copyright information about Help

Undelete for Windows

Toolbar Buttons

Undeletes the files selected in the Undelete window—if they can be undeleted

Changes the drive and/or directory

Finds deleted files by file specification and/or text strings

Sorts files by name, extension, size, deleted date and time, modified date and time, or condition

Prints the deleted file list displayed in the Undelete window

Displays file information for the most recently selected file in the Undelete window

continues

Undelete for Windows *(continued)*

File Menu

U̲ndelete	Undeletes selected files or directories displayed in the Undelete window to their original location on the disk—if they can be undeleted
Undelete t̲o...	Undeletes selected files or directories displayed in the Undelete window to a specified location on a different drive or in a different directory
Change D̲rive/ Directory...	Changes the drive and/or the directory of the deleted file list; you can then select the newly displayed files or directories to undelete
Fi̲nd Deleted File...	Finds deleted files by file specification and/or text strings
File I̲nfo...	Displays file information for the most recently selected file in the Undelete window
P̲urge Delete Sentry File	Purges files from Delete Sentry's hidden directory; once purged, a file cannot be undeleted
Print L̲ist	Prints the deleted file list displayed in the Undelete window
Printer S̲etup...	Configures printer options
E̲xit	Quits Undelete

Options Menu

S̲ort by...	Sorts files in the file list according to name, extension, size, date, or condition; you can sort files first by directory if you wish
Select b̲y Name...	Selects a group of files in the file list by filename— an alternative to individually selecting files for recovery that lets you select multiple files quickly
U̲nselect by Name...	Unselects a group of selected files displayed in the Undelete window
C̲onfigure Delete Protection...	Configures either the Delete Sentry or Delete Tracker methods of Delete Protection

Help Menu

Index	Displays a list of topics for Undelete
Keyboard	Displays a list of keyboard keys and their functions for Undelete
Glossary	Displays a list of Undelete terms; click on a term to see its meaning
Using Help	Displays a list of topics about how to use the Windows Help facility
About Undelete...	Displays version and copyright information about Undelete

COMMAND-LINE EDITING KEYS

When you enter a command at the command prompt, MS-DOS retains that command in memory. When the prompt returns, you can use the keys below to recall or modify that command. And if you run Doskey, you have access to the most recently entered command and several that preceded it—and greater editing control.

Key	Action
F1	Copies the previous command to your screen, one character at a time (one character is displayed each time you press F1)
F2	Copies the previous command to your screen, up to but not including the character you press immediately after pressing F2
F3	Copies the remainder of the previous command to your screen
F4	Deletes characters from the previous command, starting from the beginning of the command, up to but not including the character you press immediately after pressing F4
F5	Copies the current command line to the "previous command" memory, but does not carry out the command

continues

Command-Line Editing Keys *(continued)*

Key	Action
F6	Places a Ctrl+Z character (^Z) in the current command line
Left or Backspace	Deletes the character before the cursor on the current command line
Del	Deletes the character at the current cursor position
Ins	Starts insert mode so that characters you type are inserted at the current cursor position instead of replacing exisiting characters; press Ins again to cancel insert mode
Esc	Cancels the current command line without carrying it out, leaving the "previous command" memory unchanged

The following command-line editing keys are functional only when Doskey is loaded.

Key	Action
Up	Recalls the MS-DOS command used before the one displayed
Down	Recalls the MS-DOS command used after the one displayed
PgUp	Recalls the first (oldest) MS-DOS command used in the current session
PgDn	Recalls the most recent MS-DOS command used
Left	Moves the cursor back one character
Right	Moves the cursor forward one character
Ctrl+Left	Moves the cursor back one word
Ctrl+Right	Moves the cursor forward one word
Home	Moves the cursor to the beginning of the line
End	Moves the cursor to the end of the line

F7	Displays all commands stored in memory
Alt+F7	Deletes all commands stored in memory
F8	Searches for commands by text strings. Press F8 and then type the text string; commands that match are displayed one at a time, most recent one first
F9	Searches for commands by command number (Doskey assigns numbers sequentially as commands are entered)
Alt+F10	Deletes all Doskey macro definitions

 Doskey

ENVIRONMENT VARIABLES

Use environment variables to control the behavior of some programs, and to control the way MS-DOS appears and works. Environment variables can be set in your AUTOEXEC.BAT file to be defined whenever you start your computer.

Use the Set command to display, set, or remove environment variables. To display the current environment variables, type *set* at the command prompt.

COMSPEC	Identifies where COMMAND.COM is located on the disk. COMSPEC is set by the Shell command or the Command command.
CONFIG	Contains the name of the configuration selected in the startup menu if you are using multiple configurations set in your CONFIG.SYS file. You can use the CONFIG variable with a GoTo command in a batch program to execute only certain parts of the program based on your original startup selection.
COPYCMD	Specifies whether you want the Copy, Move, and XCopy commands to prompt you for confirmation before overwriting a file, whether entered from the command prompt or executed from a batch program. Use *set copycmd=/–y* to prompt you before overwriting; use *set copycmd=/y* to overwrite without prompting you. (Version 6.2)

continues

Environment Variables *(continued)*

DIRCMD   Sets the default parameters and switches for use with the Dir command. You can use any valid parameters you would normally use when typing *dir* at the command prompt or executing the Dir command in a batch file. For example, *set dircmd=/w* sets a wide display as the default whenever you type *dir*.

MSDOSDATA   Specifies the directory where configuration information is stored for the Anti-Virus and Backup programs. If MSDOSDATA is not specified, Anti-Virus and Backup look in the directory that contains the program files. If a configuration file does not exist, the program creates one.

PATH   Indicates which directories MS-DOS should search for executable (program) files. You can display the current search path by typing *path*.

PROMPT   Determines the appearance of the command prompt. Use the Prompt command to set the prompt variable.

TEMP   Specifies the directory where temporary files—created by some programs—are stored. When you exit a program normally, it deletes its temporary files. Occasionally files remain in the directory specified by TEMP; you can periodically delete any files there. Quit all programs first, including Windows and MS-DOS Shell, to avoid deleting a temporary file that is currently in use.

WINPMT   Determines the appearance of the command prompt when you open an MS-DOS Prompt session from within Windows. For example, *set winpmt=Type "exit" to return to Windows$_$p$g* will remind you that you're running MS-DOS in Windows. WINPMT does not affect the command prompt set with the PROMPT environment variable.

FILENAME EXTENSIONS

A filename extension (the three characters that follow the period in a filename) is supposed to give you a clue about what type of file you're looking at. The files included with MS-DOS (and the files created by MS-DOS commands and programs) use one of the following extensions. Other programs also use these extensions—and many, many others.

BAT Batch program; an unformatted text file that contains one or more MS-DOS commands

CAT Backup master catalog file

CHK File recovered by CHKDSK; when you use CHKDSK /F to fix disk errors, MS-DOS saves each lost chain as a file in the root directory

COM Program file

CPI Character set information file; used to load one of the character sets included with MS-DOS instead of your hardware character set

DIF Backup catalog (differential backup)

DLL Dynamic Link Library, a program file used by Windows-based applications

EXE Program file

FUL Backup catalog (full backup)

HLP Help file

INC Backup catalog (incremental backup)

INI Initialization file, which contains settings and preferences for a program

SET Setup file used by Backup to store file selections, program settings, and options

SYS Device driver; device drivers are loaded in your CONFIG.SYS file to run devices you have installed in or attached to your computer, such as monitors, modems, CD-ROM drives, and so on

continues

Filename Extensions *(continued)*

TXT	Unformatted text file
UMB	Backup files created by MemMaker

Avoiding Danger: Traveler's Advisory

Commands and Programs Not to Use When Windows Is Running

Append
Dblspace
Defrag
Emm386
FastOpen
MemMaker

Mscdex
NLSFunc
Smartdrv
Subst
VSafe

Commands and Programs Not to Use with a Compressed Drive

DiskCopy
FDisk
RAMDrive

Subst
Sys

SPECIAL CHARACTERS

. and .. directory 12
* (asterisk) 150–51
\ (backslash) 6, 131
$ (dollar sign) 54, 117, 122
/? (FastHelp) 66, 81–82
> (greater than
    sign) 106, 126, 138, 143
< (less than sign) 106, 126, 138, 143
% (percent
    sign) 80, 86–87, 113, 116–17
¦ (pipe) 118, 138
? (question mark) 150–51
; (semicolon) 127
_ (underscore) 65

A

access denied 164
allocation units, lost. See ChkDsk
    command
ANSI escape sequences 12
ANSI.SYS device driver
    about 12
    Mode command and 105
Anti-Virus program
    for MS-DOS
        about 13–15
        menus 170–71
    for Windows
        about 13–14, 70
        menus 171–72
    See also VSafe command
Append command
    about 15
    Windows and 186
applications, Windows-based .. 152
applications, MS-DOS–based .. 110
archive file attribute 69
archiving. See Backup program
Assign command 16

asterisk (*) 150–51
Attrib command 16, 125, 164
    See also file attributes
attributes, file 47, 69
AUTOEXEC.BAT
    about 17
    bypassing 23, 156
    FastOpen program and 66
    Install command in 88
    LoadHigh command in 94
    MemMaker program and 97–98
    multiple configurations and 113
    Path command and 117
    Prompt command and 122
    Set command and 133
    SMARTDrive program and ... 137
    Subst command in 140
    Undelete and 40, 41
    Verify command and 148
Automount 18, 58, 160–61
    See also DoubleSpace program
AUX device name 46

B

backslash (\) 6, 131
Backup command 130
Backup program
    about 18–21
    for Windows 70
    menus 172–174
    troubleshooting 161
bad command or
    filename 164–65
bad command interpreter 165
BAT filename extension 185
batch programs
    about 22
    Echo command in 61
    editing. (see Editor program)
    environment variables in 64
    ErrorLevel and 64
    FC command in 67

batch programs *(continued)*
  For command in 77
  GoTo command in 79
  If command in 86–88
  labels in 79
  Pause command and 118
  replaceable parameters
    in 116–17
  Shift command in 136
  See also AUTOEXEC.BAT
boot disk 23, 79, 141
booting 4, 23, 156
  See also Ctrl+Alt+Del
Break command 23
buffer, print 120
Buffers command 24, 30
byte 24, 92, 95

C

caching
  about 136–37
  CD-ROM drive and 108
  FastOpen program and 66
  See also SMARTDrive program
Call command 24
CAT filename extension 185
CD (change directory)
  command 25
CD-ROM drive
  about 25
  caching 108
  SMARTDrive and 108
  See also Mscdex command
changing directories 25
ChDir command 25
checking disks 132–33
CHK filename extension 68, 185
ChkDsk command 26, 68, 163
CHKLIST.MS files 13, 27
  See also Anti-Virus program
Choice command 28, 87–88

clean boot 156
clearing the screen 29
Cls command 29
code page 29
colors, setting 102
COM device 46, 120
COM filename extension 185
Command command
  about 29
  Exit command and 65
command history 52–55
  See also Doskey
command line
  about 5
  editing 53
  editing keys 181–83
  typing error 5
command prompt 4
COMMAND.COM 79, 135, 141
comment 127
Comp command 30
comparing
  disks 50
  files 67
  text 86–87
compressed drives
  commands not to use with .. 186
  See also DoubleSpace program
compressed files 36, 65
compressed volume file
  (CVF) 36, 56
COMSPEC environment
  variable 183
CON device 46
CONFIG environment
  variable 183
CONFIG.SYS
  about 30–31
  bypassing 23, 156
  CD-ROM drive and 25, 108
  comments in 31, 127
  Country command and 142
  device drivers in 43, 45

CONFIG.SYS *(continued)*
   DOS command and 52
   editing (*see* Editor program)
   EMM386.EXE and 63, 85
   FastOpen program and 66
   Files command in 71
   HIMEM.SYS and 85
   Include command in 88
   Install command in 88
   Interlnk command and 89
   LastDrive command in 93
   LoadHigh command in 94
   MemMaker program and .. 97–98
   memory and 97
   MenuColor command
     in 102, 103
   multiple
     configurations 80, 102, 103,
     112–13
   NumLock command in 114
   power management and .. 119–20
   RAMDrive and 124
   Rem command in 127
   Set command in 133
   setting colors in 102
   SETVER.EXE 134, 135
   Stacks command in 139
   Submenu command in 139
conventional memory. *See*
   memory
COPYCMD environment
   variable 183
Copy command
   about 32–33
   printing with 121
copying
   directories (*see* Backup com-
     mand; Replace command;
     XCopy command)
   disks 51
   files (*see* Backup command;
     Copy command; Replace com-
     mand; XCopy command)

Country command 37, 142
CPI filename extension 185
Ctrl+Alt+Del 34, 156
Ctrl+Break 23, 34, 118
Ctrl+C 23, 35, 118
current directory 35
current drive 36
cursor 5
CVF (compressed volume
   file) 36, 56

D

Date command 37
Dblspace command. *See*
   DoubleSpace program
Debug program 38
Defrag program
   about 38–39
   DoubleSpace program and 61
   menus 174–75
   Windows and 186
Del command 40
Delete Sentry 40
Delete Tracker 41
deleted files, recovering. *See* Delete
   Sentry; Delete Tracker;
   Undelete command
deleting
   directories (*see* DelTree com-
     mand; RD command)
   files 40
Deloldos command 42
DelTree command 42, 163
Device command 30, 43
device drivers
   about 44
   ANSI.SYS 12
   CONFIG.SYS and 30
   EMM386.EXE 63
   HIMEM.SYS 85
   INTERLNK.EXE 89
   memory and 99

device drivers *(continued)*
  POWER.EXE 118–20
  RAMDRIVE.SYS 124
  SETVER.EXE 134
  SMARTDRV.EXE 136–37
device names 46
DeviceHigh command ... 30, 31, 45
diagnostics 109
DIF filename extension 185
Dir command 46–48
DIRCMD environment
  variable 48, 184
directories
  . and 12
  about 49
  changing current 25
  copying 152–53
  creating 95
  deleting *(see* DelTree command;
    RD command)
  moving 107
  naming 95
  printing 47, 121
  renaming 107
  sorting 138
  viewing *(see* Dir command; Tree
    command)
directory
  parent 117
  root 131
  structure 6
disk cache 136–37
  See also SMARTDrive program
disk drive 51
disk, boot 23
DiskComp command 50
DiskCopy command
  about 51
  compressed drives and 186
disks
  about 8
  boot 79, 141
  checking 132–33

disks *(continued)*
  comparing 50
  compressing 58
  copying 51
  fixing errors 133
  formatting 78–79
  mounting compressed ... 160–61
  naming *(see* Label command;
    Vol command)
  preparing *(see* FDisk command;
    Format command; Sys com-
    mand)
  recovering 147
  sizes 76
  system 79, 141
  unformatting 147
  volume label 78, 149
  write protecting 75
  See also floppy disks
DLL filename extension 185
DMA buffer size 166
dollar sign ($) 54, 117, 122
DOS. *See* MS-DOS
DOS command 52
DOS Shell. *See* MS-DOS Shell
Doskey program
  about 52–55
  LoadHigh command and 94
  replaceable parameters
    and 116–17
DoubleGuard 55
  See also DoubleSpace program
DoubleSpace program
  about 56–61
  creating compressed drive 56
  floppy disks and 58–59
  Info command 70
  LastDrive command and 93
  menus 175–76
  mounting disks 160–61
  ScanDisk program and 132
  Windows and 60–61, 186
  See also Automount;
    DoubleGuard

drive, CD-ROM 25
drive, changing volume label 93
drive, compressed. *See*
    DoubleSpace program
drives
    about 51
    defragmenting 61
    floppy 3, 76
    hard 2, 51
    host 56
    Interlnk 89
    LastDrive command and 93
    RAM 124
    uncompressing 59
drivers. *See* device drivers

E

Echo command 61–62
Edit command. *See* Editor pro-
    gram
Editor program
    about 62–63
    menus 176–77
Edlin program 63
EMM386.EXE
    about 43, 63
    DeviceHigh and 45
    memory and 99
    UMBs and 144
    Windows and 186
    See also memory
EMS page frame 166
environment space, out of 168
environment variables
    about 64
    DIRCMD 48
    GoTo command and 80
    If command and 86
    list of 183–84
    MSDOSDATA 20
    Shell command and 135
    See also Set command

Erase command 64
ErrorLevel
    about 64–65
    If command and 87–88
escape sequences 12
EXE filename extension 185
exit code 64–65
Exit command 65
Expand command 65
expanded memory not
    available 166
expanded memory. *See* memory

F

F1 (help) 84
F5 (clean boot) 156
F7 (recall command history) 53
F8 (interactive boot) 156
F9 (recall command by line
    number) 53
FastHelp command 66, 81–82
FastOpen program
    about 66
    Windows and 186
FC command 67, 76–77
FDisk command 186
file attributes 47, 69
    See also Attrib command
file handles 71
File Manager Tools menu .. 70, 104
file specification 6, 47, 72
FILE0000.CHK 68
filename 6, 71, 72
filename extensions, list of ... 185–86
files
    about 6–7, 8–9, 68
    attributes 68
    backing up 18–21
    batch 22
    changing date and time 33
    CHK 68

files *(continued)*
  comparing 67
  compressed 65
  copying 152–53
  creating *(see* Editor)
  defined 68
  deleting 40
  editing *(see* Editor)
  listing 46–48
  lost 162
  managing 8
  moving..................................... 107
  naming 71
  printing............................. 120–21
  recovering 147, 162
  renaming 127
  restoring 21, 130, 161
  sorting text 138
  uncompressing *(see* Expand command)
  undeleting 145–46, 162
  updating 128
  viewing 144
Files command 30, 71
filter 72
Find command 72, 73–74
floppy disks
  about 75
  formatting 78–79
  mounting compressed ... 160–61
  See also disks; floppy drives
floppy drives
  about 3, 76
  troubleshooting 167–68
  See also disks; floppy disks
For command
  about 76–77
  Find command and 74
  replaceable parameters and ... 117
Format command 78–79
FUL filename extension 185
function keys, command-line
  editing.............................. 181–83

G

GoTo command 79–80
Graphics program 80–81, 121
greater than
  sign (>) 106, 126, 138, 143

H

hard disk. *See* disk drive
help 5, 81–84
hidden file attribute 69
high memory area 52, 85
high memory. *See* memory
HIMEM.SYS 30, 43, 45, 85, 99
HLP filename extension 185
HMA 52, 85
host drive 56

I

If command 86–88
INC filename extension 185
Include command 88
INI filename extension 185
Install command
  about 88
  FastOpen program and 66
interactive boot 156
Interlnk program 89–91
Intersvr program 90, 91
IO.SYS 79, 141

K

KB (kilobyte) 92
  See also MB
keyboard 2
keys, command-line
  editing................................ 181–83

kilobyte 92
  See also megabyte

Label command 92–93
labels, in batch programs 79
LastDrive command 30, 89
less than
  sign (<) 106, 126, 138, 143
LH. *See* LoadHigh command
lines, changing number of
  display 105
list device 120
LoadHigh command 94
lost allocation units. *See* ChkDsk
  command
LPT device 46, 120

macros, Doskey 52–55
MB (megabyte) 95
  See also KB
MD (make directory)
  command 95
MS-DOS, uninstalling 147
  See also Deloldos command
megabyte 95
  See also kilobyte
Mem command 96
MemMaker program
  about 97–98
  memory 99–101
  troubleshooting 157–160,
    166, 168
  Windows and 186
memory
  about 99
  checking (*see* Mem command)
  LoadHigh command and 94

memory *(continued)*
  Mem command and 96
  MemMaker program and .. 97–98
  optimizing (*see* MemMaker
    program)
  out of 168
  troubleshooting 156, 168
  types of 100–101
memory-resident
  programs 99, 101
MenuColor command 102, 112
MenuDefault
  command 102, 103, 112
[Menu] header 103, 112, 114
MenuItem command 103, 112
menus
  Anti-Virus for MS-DOS .. 170–71
  Anti-Virus for Windows .. 171–72
  Backup program 172–74
  Defrag program 174–75
  DoubleSpace program ... 175–76
  Editor program 176–77
  File Manager Tools 70
  MSD program 178–79
  Undelete for Windows ... 179–81
Microsoft Anti-Virus. *See* Anti-
  Virus program
Microsoft Backup 18–21
Microsoft Diagnostics program 109
Microsoft Tools program
  group 70, 104, 146
Microsoft Tools
  Anti-Virus program 13–15
  Backup program 18–21
Microsoft Undelete. *See* Undelete
Mirror command 104
missing command interpreter ... 165
MkDir command 95
Mode command 105–106
monitor 2
More command 106
mounting compressed
  disks 160–61

mouse 3
Move command 107
MS-DOS
    about 2–3
    booting 4–5
    starting 4–5
    uninstalling 147
    version 148
MS-DOS–based applications ... 110
MS-DOS 6 Technical Reference .. 129
MS-DOS Editor. *See* Editor
MS-DOS Help. *See* Help
MS-DOS Resource Kit 129
MS-DOS Shell 110–11, 141–42
Msav command. *See* Anti-Virus
    program
MSBackup command 18–21
Mscdex command............. 108, 186
MSD program
    about 109
    menus 178–79
MSDOS.SYS 79, 141
MSDOSDATA environment
    variable 20, 184
multiple configurations
    about 112–113
    colors and 102, 103
    GoTo command and 80
    Include command and 88
    NumLock and 114
    Submenu command and 139
multitasking. *See* MS-DOS Shell;
    TaskSwapper
NLSFunc command 186
non-system disk 167
not ready reading drive 167
NUL device 46
NumLock command 114

OLD_DOS 114
    See also Deloldos command;
        Uninstall command
out of environment space 168
out of memory 168

parameters
    about 115–16
    Doskey 54
    If command and 86
    shifting 136
parent directory 117
Path command 117
PATH environment variable ... 184
pathname 6, 65, 72, 117, 140
    See also file specification
Pause command 80, 86–87,
    116–17, 118
percent sign
    (%) 80, 86-87, 113, 116-17
pipe (¦) 138
piping
    about 118
    More command and 106
    Sort command and 138
    Type command and 144
    See also redirection
Power command 119–20
POWER.EXE 119–20
power management 119–20
print buffer 120
Print command 120–21
printer 3
printer, configuring 105–106
printing
    configuring printer 105–106
    directories 47

printing *(continued)*

    directory tree 143

    graphics 80–81

    help 84

    Print command 120–21

    See also Copy command, redi-

        rection

print screen 121

PRN device 46, 120

Prompt command 4, 12, 122–23

PROMPT environment

    variable 184

PrtSc 121

QBasic 123

question mark (?) 150–51

quick format 78

RAM. *See* memory

RAMDrive 93, 124, 186

RD (remove directory)

    command 125

read-only attribute. *See* Attrib

    command; file attributes

rebooting 156

redirection

    about 126

    Doskey macros and 54–55

    More command and 106

    printing with 61, 121

    Sort command 138

    Tree command 143

    See also piping

Rem command 127

remark 127

Ren (rename) command 127

Rename command 127

Replace command 128–29

replaceable parameters. *See*

    parameters

Resource Kit, MS-DOS 129

Restore command 21, 130, 161

    See also Undelete command;

        Unformat command

RmDir command 125

root directory 6, 131

ScanDisk program 68, 132–33

screen lines, changing

    number of 105

screen, clearing 29

search path. *See* Path command

semicolon (;) 127

serial number 133

serial port, configuring 105

server. *See* Interlnk command;

    Intersvr command

Set command 133

SET filename extension 185

set of filenames 76

SetVer device driver 134

Share command 135

Shell. *See* MS-DOS Shell

Shell command 135

Shift command 136

SMARTDrive program

    about 136–37

    buffers and 24

    CD-ROM drive and 25, 108

    Windows and 186

Smartmon command 137

Sort command 72, 126, 138

spooler 120

Stacks command 139

startup 4

startup menu, setting colors in .. 102

subdirectories 6, 139

Submenu command 112, 139
Subst command
   about 140
   compressed drives and 186
   LastDrive command and 93
   pathnames and 117
   Windows and 186
Supplemental Disk 110, 129, 140
surface scan 132
switching programs 142
Sys command 141, 186
SYS filename extension 185
system disk 79, 141
system file attribute 69
system unit 2–3

T

Task Swapper 91, 111, 141–42
Technical Reference, MS-DOS 6 . 129
TEMP environment variable ... 184
terminate-and-stay-resident programs. *See* memory-resident
   programs
text
   comparing 86–87
   finding 73–74
   sorting 138
Time command 142
Tools. *See* Microsoft Tools
Tools menu, File Manager ... 70, 104
tree 7
Tree command 143
TSRs. *See* memory-resident programs
TXT filename extension 186
Type command 144

U

UMB filename extension 186
UMBs 45, 144
uncompressing
   drives 59
   files 65
Undelete
   command 145–46, 156, 162
   See also Delete Sentry; Delete
     Tracker
Undelete for Windows
   about 146
   menus 179–81
underscore (_) 65
Unformat command 147
uninstalling MS-DOS 147
   See also Deloldos command
upper memory area 45, 144
   See also memory

V

variables. *See* environment vari-
   ables; parameters
Ver command 148
Verify command 148
version table 134
virus. *See* Anti-Virus program;
   VSafe command
Vol command 149
volume label 78, 92, 149
VSafe command 149–50, 186
   See also Anti-Virus program

W

wildcards
   about 9, 150–51
   copying and 32

wildcards *(continued)*

  file specifications and 72

  For command and 74

  printing with 120

  renaming with 127

WINA20.386 152

Windows

  Anti-Virus

    program 14, 70, 171–72

  Backup program ... 19, 70, 172–74

  commands not to use with 186

  File Manager Tools menu 70, 104

  Intersvr command and 91

  Microsoft Tools

    program group 104

  SMARTDrive and 137

Windows *(continued)*

  Undelete 146, 179–81

  WINPMT environment

    variable 184

Windows-based

  applications 152, 156

WINPMT environment

  variable 184

write protection 75

X

XCopy command 152–53

XMS memory. *See* memory

The manuscript for this book was prepared and submitted to Microsoft Press in electronic form. Text files were prepared using Microsoft Word 6.0 for Windows. Pages were composed by Siechert & Wood using PageMaker for Windows, with text in Minion and display type in Copperplate. Composed pages were delivered to the printer as electronic prepress files.

COVER DESIGNER
Rebecca Geisler

COVER ILLUSTRATOR
Eldon Doty

COVER COLOR SEPARATOR
Color Service, Inc.

INTERIOR TEXT DESIGNER
The Understanding Business

PRINCIPAL TYPOGRAPHER
Paula Kausch

PRINCIPAL PROOFREADER/COPY EDITOR
Carl Siechert

INDEXER
Stan DeGulis

Printed on recycled paper stock.